Paul on Trial

Paul on Trial

by
John MacArthur, Jr.

WORD OF GRACE COMMUNICATIONS
P.O. Box 4000
Panorama City, CA 91412

All Scripture quotations, unless noted otherwise, are from the *New Scofield Reference Bible*, King James Version. Copyright © 1967 by Oxford University Press, Inc. Reprinted by permission.

The use of selected references from various versions of the Bible in this publication does not necessarily imply publisher endorsement of the versions in their entirety.

Library of Congress Cataloging in Publication Data

MacArthur, John.
    Paul on trial.

    (John MacArthur's Bible studies)
    Includes index.
    1. Bible. N.T.   Acts XXIV, 1-XXVI, 32—Criticism,
interpretation, etc.   2. Paul, the Apostle, Saint—
Trials, litigation, etc.   I. Title.   II. Series:
MacArthur, John.   Bible studies.
BS2625.2.M27   1986   226'.606   86-12722
ISBN 0-8024-5131-4 (pbk.)

1 2 3 4 5 6 Printing / GB / Year 91 90 89 88 87 86

Printed in the United States of America

Contents

These Bible studies are taken from messages delivered by Pastor-Teacher John MacArthur, Jr., at Grace Community Church in Panorama City, California. These messages have been combined into an 8-tape album entitled *Paul on Trial*. You may purchase this series either in an attractive vinyl cassette album or as individual cassettes. To purchase these tapes, request the album *Paul on Trial* or ask for the tapes by their individual GC numbers. Please consult the current price list; then, send your order, making your check payable to:

WORD OF GRACE COMMUNICATIONS
P.O. Box 4000
Panorama City, CA 91412

Or, call the following toll-free number:
1-800-55-GRACE

1
Paul's Trial Before Felix—Part 1
The Case Against Paul

Outline
Introduction
A. Felix: The Tragedy of Lost Opportunity
  1. His opportunity
  2. His rule
B. Paul: The Triumph of Providential Intervention
  1. The setting
  2. The specifics
  3. The solution
Lesson
I. The Prosecution (vv. 1-9)
  A. The Accusers (vv. 1-4)
    1. Their identification (v. 1)
      a) Ananias
      b) The elders
      c) Tertullus
    2. Their flattery (vv. 2-4)
      a) The hearing begins (v. 2a)
      b) The flattery begins (vv. 2b-4)
        (1) Great peace (v. 2b)
        (2) Great deeds (v. 2c)
        (3) Great thankfulness (v. 3)
        (4) Great brevity (v. 4)
  B. The Accusation (vv. 5-9)
    1. False charges (vv. 5-6a)
      a) Sedition (v. 5a)
        (1) The evidence
        (2) The exaggeration
        (3) The evaluation
      b) Sectarianism (v. 5b)
        (1) The contemptuous title
        (2) The troublesome faction
      c) Sacrilege (v. 6a)

2. False testimony (vv. 6*b*-9)
  a) The scriptural problem
  b) The contextual resolution
    (1) The request (vv. 6*b*-8)
    (2) The assent (v. 9)

Introduction

Some passages in Scripture are theological, while others are historical narrative. Acts follows the pattern of the latter. The gospels are both doctrinal and historical, but the book of Acts is a running historical narrative. Doctrine appears rather sporadically—it is more often implied than stated.

Acts 24 is the story of one man. Yet it is as much the story of an evil man—Felix—as it is the story of a good man—Paul.

A. Felix: The Tragedy of Lost Opportunity

Felix was evil in every sense of the word. He was a corrupt official. His wife Drusilla married a king when she was fifteen, but Felix lusted for her, seduced her, and stole her from her husband. First-century Roman historian Tacitus said that Felix "exercised the powers of a king in the spirit of a slave" (*Histories* 5:9).

1. His opportunity

Felix is one of the great illustrations of lost opportunity. Nineteenth-century Kansas Senator J. J. Ingalls wrote these words describing opportunity:

Master of human destinies am I!
  Fame, love and fortune on my footsteps wait.
  Cities and fields I walk; I penetrate
Deserts and seas remote, and passing by
  Hovel and mart and palace, soon or late
  I knock unbidden once at every gate!
If sleeping, wake; if feasting, rise before
  I turn away. It is the hour of fate,
  And they who follow me reach every state
Mortals desire, and conquer every foe
Save death; but those who doubt or hesitate,
  Condemned to failure, penury and woe,
Seek me in vain and uselessly implore.
I answer not, and I return no more!

The greatest story of lost opportunity in the history of man was Judas. He was condemned to hell for his

2

unbelief. What might Judas have been? He could have been one of the twelve apostles of the Lamb, reigning in the kingdom. He might have been one of the twelve foundations of the heavenly Jerusalem or one of the twelve stones on the breastplate of the eternal High Priest. He might have been one of the glorified saints of all eternity. But what was he? He was a traitor, thief, and hypocrite. Jesus Christ said of him, "Good were it for that man if he had never been born" (Mark 14:21). Judas lived with the Son of God but forfeited his opportunity.

There was another man like Judas, and his name was Felix. The apostle Paul lived in his house for two years. There wasn't another man like Paul, yet Felix rejected all that Paul stood for and proclaimed.

2. His rule

Antonius Felix was this man's full name. He was the governor of Judea, following in the infamous line of Pilate. He ruled Judea from A.D. 52 to 60. He acquired his position because his brother Pallus was a friend of emperor Claudius—not because he had any leadership qualities. His reign as procurator was marked by trouble. The Sicarii, who were professional Jewish agitators and assassins, were a problem during his rule. Felix did manage to quell some riots. But when he stopped one particular riot, he killed many people and alienated the Jews he was trying to protect. In Acts 24, Felix appears not only as indecisive and procrastinating but also as a coward.

B. Paul: The Triumph of Providential Intervention

1. The setting

The book of Acts records the history of the church from the Day of Pentecost until it brought its message to the great capital of the world, Rome. During those early years, many exciting things happened. Two people dominated: Peter during the first few years and Paul during the last years. Acts 24 takes place in the midst of the story of Paul—the man who took the gospel to the Gentiles. He took three tours to Gentile countries, and as we come to Acts 24, he is finishing his third tour. He was no longer a free man; he was now a prisoner.

When Paul arrived in Jerusalem at the conclusion of his third tour, he tried to pacify the Jewish Christians by

3

going to the Temple. Although he was a Christian, he wanted to show them that he wasn't anti-Jewish because he still believed in some of the customs of Israel. While he was in the Temple, some Jews from Asia Minor saw him and tried to kill him (Acts 21:27-30). Paul had won so many Jews to Christ in Asia Minor that he upset those who had not come to Christ. So when they saw him in the Temple, they attacked him.

As we come to Acts 24, Paul arrives in Caesarea. His ministry as a prisoner took place in three cities: Jerusalem, Caesarea, and Rome. He spent only a few days in Jerusalem, but he spent a few years in Caesarea before he was sent to Rome.

2.   The specifics

A riot started when Paul entered the Temple in Jerusalem. A tribune named Claudius Lysias was the captain at Fort Antonia. He was responsible for keeping the peace in Jerusalem as the representative for Felix, who was the procurator of the territory of Judea. Claudius Lysias rescued Paul. He assumed that Paul must have done something terrible for the people to be so adamant in their effort to kill him. Claudius tried to get an accusation against Paul, but he couldn't (Acts 21:33-34). So he decided to torture Paul. As he was being stretched out to be scourged, Paul informed a soldier standing nearby that he was a Roman citizen (Acts 22:24-25). In a panic they cut him loose, because to scourge a Roman was a crime according to Roman law. Since Claudius still did not have an accusation, he decided to take Paul before the Sanhedrin. But when Paul appeared before the Jewish council, the leaders began to fight about him. And still Claudius didn't have an accusation.

3.   The solution

Claudius was in a difficult situation. As a Roman, he had a sense of justice. Also, he wanted to keep his job, so he couldn't execute a Roman citizen who wasn't guilty of anything. But in an area like Jerusalem, which was a hotbed of Judaism, he had to be sure that he pacified the Jewish people. If he didn't, he might have a riot on his hands. Worse, he might lose his job and possibly his life because he wasn't able to keep the political situation from turning into revolutionary proportions. Claudius didn't want to violate Roman justice, and he didn't want to cause problems with the Jewish people.

When Claudius realized that he would be unable to accuse Paul, he had Paul removed out of Jerusalem in the middle of the night to avoid the burden of a decision. Four-hundred-seventy Roman soldiers escorted Paul to Caesarea (Acts 23:23). You can imagine that Claudius was glad he had turned his problem over to Felix. But now Felix had the same problem Claudius previously had. He also had a sense of justice and obligation to Rome. He couldn't kill a Roman citizen without an accusation, and he also had to pacify the Jews. That kind of dilemma ultimately destroyed Pilate. He repeatedly said he found no fault in Jesus, but he let the Jewish leaders crucify Him because they had pressured him. They implied that they would report Pilate to Caesar for allowing a seditionary to live (John 19:12). Felix responded in much the same way Pilate did.

Lesson

There are three ways to look at Paul's trial before Felix in Acts 24. You can look at what Paul is doing, what God is doing, and what Felix is doing. Like so many passages in Scripture, this one is like a diamond—it has many facets. You could use this passage to teach about Paul's attitude in the midst of a trial. You could use it to teach about the tragedy of procrastination, as I intend to do. You could use it to teach about the providence of God. And you could use it to teach about the hatred of unbelief and the hardness of men's hearts when they turn against Christ.

The passage divides itself into three simple parts: the prosecution, the defense, and the verdict.

I. THE PROSECUTION (vv. 1-9)

Claudius Lysias sent a letter to Felix explaining the situation concerning Paul. In effect Claudius said, "As far as I can see, this situation is a matter of Jewish theology. Paul hasn't done anything for which he should be put in jail or killed" (Acts 23:26-30). Claudius stamped Paul as innocent. Then he told Paul's accusers that if they wanted to pursue their case, they would have to go to Caesarea, which they did. You would think that the Jewish leaders would be content in having Paul out of Jerusalem, but they wanted him dead. He was a threat to them because he undermined their security. They loved their spiritual prestige and prominence. But Paul called them hypocrites. The very One they had deemed a blasphemer and executed, Paul preached as Jesus the Christ, the Son of God—the Messiah. Paul was doing the same thing Jesus had done—he was destroying their theology, and they couldn't tolerate that. Paul was also winning many Jews to Christ, and that was creating problems for the other Jews. So they took the sixty-mile trip down to Caesarea to accuse him.

A. The Accusers (vv. 1-4)

1. Their identification (v. 1)

   "And after five days Ananias, the high priest, descended with the elders, and with a certain orator, named Tertullus, who informed the governor against Paul."

   a) Ananias—Ananias was a corrupt high priest. He saw Paul as a threat, so he wanted to get rid of him. That's why he was part of the entourage that went to accuse Paul.

   b) The elders—The elders were key leaders of the Sanhedrin, the supreme court of Israel.

   c) Tertullus—Ananias and the elders didn't want to accuse themselves, so they hired a professional case reader by the name of Tertullus. He was probably well versed in the legal procedure of Rome and spoke eloquent Latin. Verse 1 says that he "informed the governor." The high priest and the elders stood silently while Tertullus did the talking.

2. Their flattery (vv. 2-4)

   It was very common for orators in those days to do what Tertullus did. In verses 2-4 he lays the flattery on thick. The Latin description of what he did is *Captatio Benevolentiae*. That could be freely translated as a "soft soap job." Tertullus buttered up Felix with flattery. There wasn't much good that could be said about Felix, so Tertullus spoke in generalities. But that was a common approach to obtaining a favorable hearing. Felix knew what Tertullus said wasn't true, but he liked to hear it anyway. That is true of Herod in Acts 12:21-22. As he sat on his throne and gave a speech, the people said that he wasn't a man but a god. Herod loved receiving such praise even though he had to know it wasn't true. So Tertullus flattered Felix, even though the governor was intelligent enough to know that the Jewish people hated him.

a) The hearing begins (v. 2*a*)

"And when he was called forth, Tertullus began to accuse him [Paul]."

We can't be sure if the hearing was formal or informal, but there is a clue that it was informal because Felix decided to defer the case to a later date according to verse 22. So Felix called Tertullus, who began his accusation.

b) The flattery begins (vv. 2*b*-4)

(1) Great peace (v. 2*b*)

"Seeing that by thee we enjoy great quietness."

Tertullus began by telling Felix that he had brought peace. Yet Felix had made no contribution to Roman peace at all. The only occasion in which Felix brought any peace was when he stopped a riot that shouldn't have started in the first place. And he did such a bad job of it that he alienated everyone. He hadn't done anything that contributed to peace; Tertullus was just flattering him. Many of the Jewish people didn't see the Pax Romanus as peace at all. Calgacus, a chieftain who fought the Romans, said that where the Romans "make a desolation, they call it 'peace'" (Tacitus, *Life of Agricola*, 29-30). It may have been peace for Rome, but it was oppression for everyone else.

(2) Great deeds (v. 2*c*)

"And that very worthy deeds are done unto this nation by thy provision."

I got out twelve different books to try to find one good thing Felix did, and I couldn't find one. Whatever good Tertullus said Felix did history didn't record. Notice that Tertullus offered no specifics, only generalities. Felix had driven off an Egyptian impostor, which ignited a revolution. He did quell a few riots. But he certainly passed no reforms of any consequence. He did many bad things. He assassinated Jonathan, the high priest, because he didn't like him (Josephus, *Antiquities*, 20.8.5). That was not the way to become popular with the Jews. The historian

Tacitus said that he "believed himself free to commit any crime" (*Annals* 12:53). In other words, he thought he could do any evil and get away with it. Tacitus also said that he indulged in every kind of barbarity and lust (*Histories* 5:9). I don't believe Felix had done very worthy deeds.

(3) Great thankfulness (v. 3)

"We accept it always, and in all places, most noble Felix, with all thankfulness."

Tertullus emphasized his statement with "always" and "all." I can imagine the Jewish leaders staring in disbelief. They could never have said what Tertullus did with a straight face. I know Felix didn't believe it. I think he enjoyed listening to the flattery because he knew the Jewish leaders had to stand there and endure what Tertullus said about him. There was certainly nothing noble about Felix.

(4) Great brevity (v. 4)

"Nothwithstanding, that I be not further tedious unto thee, I beseech thee that thou wouldest hear us of thy clemency [yieldedness—a willingness to give place to another] a few words."

Tertullus claimed that he didn't want to continue to recite the things he had been saying so as not to be tedious to Felix. The truth probably was that he didn't have anything more to say. The idea of not being tedious was common. There is historical evidence that orators often began their speech by saying that it would be brief. They said that so they could elicit the concentration of the hearer at the beginning. Their speeches didn't always turn out to be brief, but it was a good way to win immediate attention.

Felix enjoyed the flattery of Tertullus because the Jewish leaders had to listen to it. But that was Tertullus's job, and he did it well.

B. The Accusation (vv. 5-9)

The accusation falls into three categories: sedition, a violation of Roman law; sectarianism, a violation of Jewish law; and sacrilege, a violation of God Himself.

1. False charges (vv. 5-6*a*)

   a) Sedition (v. 5*a*)

   "For we have found this man a pestilent fellow, and
   a mover of sedition among all the Jews throughout
   the world."

   Sedition could be translated "treason." If they could
   make that charge stick, they would get him in deep
   trouble with the Romans. The phrase "pestilent fellow" in verse 5 translates as "a nuisance." In modern-
   day vernacular, they considered Paul to be a pain in
   the neck. Now that wasn't an accusation; that was
   just a general statement reflecting their attitude toward Paul. They went on to define the three areas in
   which they thought he was such a problem.

   (1) The evidence

   First, they accused Paul of sedition against the
   government. Verse 5 says, "We have found this
   man a mover of sedition among all the Jews
   throughout the world." They accused Paul of
   causing Jews to revolt against Rome. Treason,
   insurrection, and riots were happening all over
   the world. Actually, that accusation had some
   basis in fact. Paul didn't stir up riots, but he was
   around when many of them occurred. He would
   preach a sermon, and then someone would get
   excited and stir up a riot. If the Jewish leaders had
   any evidence that Tertullus could have used to
   support their accusation, it was this one fact. But
   Paul could never have been justifiably accused,
   although they had the potential to make the
   accusation stick if they could twist the truth. The
   Romans were paranoid about revolutions, insur-
   rections, and riots in their foreign territories, and
   they placed rulers and soldiers in those areas to
   keep the peace.

   (2) The exaggeration

   Verse 5 says that Paul was "a mover of sedition
   among all the Jews throughout the world." Tertullus doesn't name any specific riot. Why? If he
   had referred to a riot in any specific area, the
   responsibility for the case would have been removed from Felix's jurisdiction. They would

have had to transfer Paul to the ruler of that area. In Acts 23:34 Paul is asked what province he is from, and he tells them Cilicia. When he said that, Felix recognized that as his jurisdiction. Tertullus was purposely vague so that Paul wouldn't be transferred. The Jewish leaders wanted an immediate decision against Paul. So they accused him of leading sedition among all the Jews throughout the world. That was a false accusation of treason. The people who created dissension in response to what Paul was preaching were actually responsible.

This particular accusation was common in ancient times. Petty tyrants and tyrannical emperors used the concept of sedition or treason at will to execute anyone who disagreed with them.

The Acquittal of Christianity

Throughout the book of Acts, Christians were put on trial for preaching Christ. The Holy Spirit recorded the features of those trials in great detail. Why did the Holy Spirit tell us every detail? Why didn't He give a general description and follow it with some doctrine? There are many trials described in the book of Acts, such as Paul before Gallio, Sergius Paulus, Felix, Festus, and Agrippa, and Peter and John before the Sanhedrin. Why did the Lord include the details of those trials? Throughout history, the church in the early years of Christianity was often condemned on the basis that it was a treasonous, revolutionary movement. The Holy Spirit was careful to record the details of each trial mentioned in the book of Acts because in every case it is abundantly clear that they were innocent of any violation of civil law.

Christianity is not political treason. The Bible is explicit about that. Jesus said, "Render, therefore, unto Caesar the things which are Caesar's" (Matt. 22:21). In Romans 13:1 the apostle Paul says, "The powers that be are ordained of God." Peter said to submit to kings, governors, and the police (1 Pet. 2:13-14). Christians are not political insurrectionists; they should be law-abiding citizens. Only when you live in a society that makes laws that violate the laws of God do you have the right to choose whether to obey God or men, and you should choose to obey God. But that's the exception. Judges like Gallio, Sergius Paulus, and Felix exonerated Christians. Luke made that clear in the book of Acts so that,

10

particularly in those early centuries, Christianity would not be branded as political insurrection.

(3) The evaluation

I don't think Felix believed the Jewish leaders' accusation of insurrection. Claudius Lysias had already written a letter to Felix about it (Acts 23:25-30). In his letter he said, "I perceived [Paul] to be accused of questions of their law, but to have nothing laid to his charge worthy of death or bonds" (v. 29). In other words, "It isn't a legal matter for us to consider; it's strictly a theological issue between them." I think Felix believed his own tribune, or he wouldn't have had Claudius in that position if he didn't think the man was capable. Felix accepted the Jewish leaders' accusation even though he knew it was a lie.

The accusation began with a vague charge, which was inadmissible as any kind of evidence.

b) Sectarianism (v. 5b)

"A ringleader of the sect of the Nazarenes."

The Jewish leaders now accused Paul of heresy—of belonging to the sect of the Nazarenes.

(1) The contemptuous title

The name "Nazarene" was originally a term of derision, as was the term "Christian." The term "Nazarene" started because Jesus of Nazareth was called the Nazarene. So people who identified with Jesus came to be known as Nazarenes. During the time of Jesus, this popular saying was reiterated by Nathanael, "Can any good thing come out of Nazareth?" (John 1:46). It was considered to be an uneducated, backward town. When the people who followed Jesus were called Nazarenes, that was a slur. Jesus was called "Jesus of Nazareth" six times in Acts, but this is the only time the people who followed Him were called Nazarenes. Apparently it was a popular term because Tertullus did not bother to explain it to Felix—he assumed Felix understood its meaning.

11

(2) The troublesome faction

During this time, there were various messianic factions, most of which didn't believe Jesus was the Messiah. Those factions were troublesome to Rome. The faction of the Nazarenes would have been classified with the other messianic factions by Rome, so they could have been perceived as a threat. When Tertullus called Paul a ringleader of the sect of the Nazarenes, he was identifying Paul with the troublesome messianic offshoots of Judaism. The Jewish leaders were accusing him of heresy—of being anti-Jewish.

c) Sacrilege (v. 6a)

"Who also hath gone about to profane the temple."

To the Jews, the Temple was sacred. The laws of the Temple were binding. There was an outer court, and the Gentiles could enter it. But they could not go past the barricade into the inner part of the Temple. Signs were posted to that effect. Archaeologists have found remnants of those signs so that we know what they said. If a Gentile went into the inner part of the Temple, he would pay with his life. It was such a serious violation of Jewish law that the Romans allowed the Jewish people to have the right of capital punishment for that offense—and for that offense only. Remember that the Jewish leaders had to get the Romans to crucify Christ. They had no right to take a life except when the sacredness of the Temple was violated.

When Paul was in the Temple, the Jews from Asia Minor who saw him there accused him of bringing a Gentile into the inner court (Acts 21:28). He hadn't done that, but they accused him of it. They even tried to kill Paul. But that was a ridiculous attempt because the law said that the Gentile who entered was to be killed, not the one who brought him in. So the facts were twisted. But in Acts 24:6 they back off that accusation. Instead of accusing Paul of bringing a Gentile into the inner court, they accused him of attempting to profane the Temple. They didn't say he did it, just that he tried to do it. Why would they back off their original charge? Because they couldn't prove it. And it couldn't be proved because Paul didn't do it. They couldn't find any witnesses. But there was also no way to prove that he didn't try to do it. That was a safe accusation. The Jewish leaders thought if the accusation was vague enough, Felix might have Paul executed.

Defending a Square Inch of Religion

"Religious" people can often be the most immoral and unethical of people. Many evil things have been perpetrated in the name of Christianity. For example, during the Crusades, "Christians" marched across Europe to take the holy places from the Turks. As they went, they slaughtered Jews along the way so that the Jews wouldn't contest possession of those holy places. It was all supposedly done in the name of Christ. You can understand why some Jewish people have a hard time with Christianity—they know history. They know that Germany was the birthplace of the Reformation and the home of Martin Luther. And they don't see that Christianity had much of an effect on the Germans, at least not during the Holocaust.

Religious wars are still going on. Catholics and Protestants are still killing each other in the name of Christ. You and I understand that that's not true Christianity, but does the world? It's difficult to connect honest morality with religion. True ethics and morality come from a true relationship with God. Apart from that, religious people can be as criminal as anyone and maybe more so when they set out to defend their square inch of religion. So we shouldn't be surprised to find the religious people in Acts 24 wanting to kill an innocent man in the name of God. They so desperately wanted Paul dead that they brought false accusations against him.

2. False testimony (vv. 6b-9)

   a) The scriptural problem

   Acts 24:6 poses an interesting problem. Some of the ancient mansucripts do not include the end of verse 6, all of verse 7, and the first part of verse 8. That is known as a problem of lower criticism—trying to determine which text is right. Certain principles are used to determine which one is right, but this is a difficult case. The *New American Standard Bible* marks verses 6b-8a in brackets.

13

b) The contextual resolution

I'm not an expert in this area, but in looking at it from a textual standpoint, I lean towards leaving those verses in the text. Let's assume first that those verses aren't in the text. Verses 6 and 8 would read this way: "Who also hath gone about to profane the temple; by examining of whom thyself mayest take knowledge of all these things, of which we accuse him." With the middle section left out, whom does the "examining of whom" in verse 8 refer to? It would have to refer to Paul. So Tertullus would be saying, "Paul has profaned the Temple. If you'll examine him, you'll find that that is true." I have a problem with that reasoning. If Felix examined Paul, he wouldn't find that it was true because Paul didn't profane the Temple. Why would the lawyer tell Felix that all he had to do to get the truth was ask Paul? It wouldn't make any sense because Paul would not have agreed with Tertullus. Let's see how the text reads with verses 6*b*-8*a* intact.

(1) The request (vv. 6*b*-8)

"Whom we took, and would have judged according to our law. But the chief captain, Lysias, came upon us, and with great violence took him away out of our hands, commanding his accusers to come unto thee; by examining of whom [Lysias] thyself mayest take knowledge of all these things, of which we accuse him."

Whom does the "whom" refer to? Lysias. That makes sense. Acts 24:22 says, "When Felix heard these things . . . he deferred them, and said, When Lysias, the chief captain, shall come down, I will determine your case." Felix wanted to hear testimony from Claudius Lysias. So Tertullus in effect says, "I've given you the accusations. If you want corroboration, get it from your chief captain. We were trying to carry out justice when Lysias took Paul away and commanded us to come down to you. Why don't you check with him and see if that isn't so?" In verse 22 Felix says he will. But he never did.

(2) The assent (v. 9)

"And the Jews also assented, saying that these things were so."

One elder after another perjured himself. They called themselves lovers of God and lovers of the law, yet they blatantly lied to preserve their religion and to execute a man they didn't want around.

Only the Holy Make Waves

The accusations brought against Paul are a clear illustration of what a Christian should expect. If a Christian lives a godly life in the face of an ungodly world, he is going to make waves.

1. 2 Timothy 3:12—Paul said, "Yea, and all that will live godly in Christ Jesus shall suffer persecution." If you're going to live a godly life in the midst of an ungodly society, you will receive some flak. That's to be expected. If you're not receiving any flak, maybe you're not living a godly life.

2. 1 Peter 3:14-16—Peter said, "If ye suffer for righteousness' sake, happy are ye; and be not afraid of their terror, neither be troubled, but sanctify the Lord God in your hearts, and be ready always to give an answer to every man that asketh you a reason of the hope that is in you, with meekness and fear, having a good conscience, that, whereas they speak evil of you, as of evildoers, they may be ashamed that falsely accuse your good manner of life in Christ." Peter is saying two things: one, have a blameless life; and two, have a clear testimony.

3. Matthew 5:11—Jesus said, "Blessed are ye, when men shall revile you, and persecute you, and shall say all manner of evil against you falsely."

Focusing on the Facts

1. Explain why Judas's life can be considered one of the greatest stories of lost opportunity (see pp. 2-3).
2. Describe the rule of Felix (see p. 3).
3. Why did Paul go to the Temple after he arrived in Jerusalem following his third tour? What happened while he was there (Acts 21:27-30; see pp. 3-4)?
4. Describe what Claudius Lysias did with Paul after he had rescued him (Acts 21:33-34; 22:24-25; see pp. 4-5).

5. What was the problem that faced Claudius? How did he finally resolve it (see pp. 4-5)?
6. Who were Paul's accusers (see p. 6)?
7. What kind of approach did Tertullus use with Felix in presenting the accusations? Describe it (see pp. 6-8).
8. What were the three accusations brought against Paul (see p. 8)?
9. When Tertullus brought the first accusation, why couldn't he name any specific riot that had been started by Paul (see pp. 9-10)?
10. Why did the Holy Spirit record the trials of Christians in the book of Acts with such detail (see p. 10)?
11. What kind of citizens are Christians to be (see p. 10)?
12. How was the term *Nazarene* used during the first century (see p. 11)?
13. Explain how the group of believers called "Nazarenes" could be conceived as a threat to Rome (see p. 12).
14. Describe the seriousness of a Gentile entering into the inner court of the Temple (see p. 12).
15. How did the Jewish leaders change their original accusation from Acts 21:28? Why did they do that (see pp. 12-13)?
16. Explain why Acts 24:6b-8a should be left in the text rather than being taken out (see pp. 13-14).
17. What will happen to the Christian who lives a godly life in the face of an ungodly world (see p. 15)?

Pondering the Principles

1. Both Judas and Felix serve as examples of men who lost their opportunity to embrace Jesus Christ as their Savior and Lord. Perhaps you know people who have been exposed to the gospel but balk at it. Take this time to pray that they might not lose their opportunity to receive Christ. Ask God to soften their hearts and convict them of their sin.

2. There are many trials of believers in the book of Acts that acquit believers of wrongdoing. Read through Acts, and make a list of each of those trials. Record the details that prove the innocence of the believers who are on trial. Thank God for His providence in taking care of each of His children.

3. When a Christian lives a godly life in this world, he will face some kind of opposition. Yet that is all part of God's plan. Read 1 Peter 3:14-16. According to verse 14, what happens when you are persecuted for the sake of righteousness? What kind of human

response should be avoided? According to verse 15, what must believers do before they can respond in the appropriate manner to persecution? How should believers respond when they are confronted about their beliefs? Are you responding in the right way? If not, examine the hope that is in you. Make sure you know the facts of the gospel message so you can communicate them to those who ask you.

2
Paul's Trial Before Felix—Part 2
Paul's Defense Begun

Outline

Introduction
A. The Testimony of Postponement
    1. By Felix
    2. By the Athenians
    3. By some potential disciples
       a) Excuse #1
       b) Excuse #2
       c) Excuse #3
B. The Tragedy of Postponement
    1. Hardened by constant rejection
       a) Hebrews 3:7-15
       b) Luke 13:23-25
    2. Abandoned by God

Review
The Prosecution (vv. 1-9)
Lesson
II. The Defense (vv. 10-21)
   A. Recognizing the Assistance (v. 10)
     1. A divine lawyer (v. 10*a*)
     2. A competent judge (v. 10*b*)
   B. Responding to the Accusations (vv. 11-21)
     1. Sedition (vv. 11-13)
       a) No time (v. 11)
         (1) The period of the vow
         (2) The purpose of the vow
       b) No riot (v. 12)
         (1) Additional defenses
           (*a*) Acts 25:8
           (*b*) Acts 28:17
         (2) Avoided dialogue

        (a) Relieved of the responsibility

        (b) Revealed by the Lord

    c) No proof (v. 13)

  2. Sectarianism (vv. 14-16)

    a) Paul's clear confession (vv. 14-15)

      (1) The conflict

      (2) The convictions

        (a) Worship of God

        (b) Belief in the law and the prophets

          i) Paul's implication

          ii) Paul's identification

        (c) Hope of the resurrection

    b) Paul's clear conscience (v. 16)

Introduction

A. The Testimony of Postponement

  1. By Felix

Acts 24:24-25 gives a graphic illustration of the tragedy of postponing a decision about Christ: "After certain days, when Felix came with his wife, Drusilla, who was a Jewess, he sent for Paul, and heard him concerning the faith in Christ. And as he reasoned of righteousness, self-control, and judgment to come, Felix trembled, and answered, Go thy way for this time; when I have a convenient season, I will call for thee." But there never was a convenient season for Felix.

  2. By the Athenians

Paul spoke to the Athenians about Christ on the Areopagus, which was the highest court of Athens. Acts 17:32 says, "When they heard of the resurrection of the dead, some mocked; and others said, We will hear thee again of this matter." As far as we know, they never did.

  3. By some potential disciples

Jesus gave us a series of comments on discipleship in Luke 9. Three would-be disciples appeared on the scene, but none of them followed the Lord. All of them failed the requirements.

    a) Excuse #1

Verse 57 says, "It came to pass that, as they went on the way, a certain man said unto him, Lord, I will follow thee wherever thou goest." That sounds good. He didn't even put any conditions on his following Him. But verse 58 says, "Jesus said unto him, Foxes have holes, and birds of the air have nests, but the Son of man hath not where to lay his head." Why did Jesus say that? The implication is that the man had a materialistic motive. He undoubtedly realized, or at least hoped, that Jesus was the Messiah. He had the same problem Judas did—he wanted to follow Jesus from the standpoint of ambition. That's why Jesus told him he wouldn't be as well off as foxes or birds because He didn't have worldly goods. The man never followed. He disqualified himself because of his materialistic motive.

b)   Excuse #2

Verse 59 says, "He said unto another, Follow me. But he said, Lord, permit me first to go and bury my father." But the man's father wasn't even dead yet. He was saying, "I'll follow you as soon as I collect my inheritance." That implied a lack of faith on his part. He didn't want to preach about the kingdom without any money to support himself. He didn't believe God could supply his needs. Verse 60 says, "Jesus said unto him, Let the dead bury their dead [let the spiritual dead take care of the physical dead]; but go thou and preach the kingdom of God." Our Lord promises that if you seek the kingdom of God, all the things you need will be given to you (Matt. 6:33). This man had a materialistic motive combined with a lack of faith.

c)   Excuse #3

Verse 61 says, "And another also said, Lord, I will follow thee; but let me first go bid them farewell, who are at home at my house. And Jesus said unto him, No man, having put his hand to the plough, and looking back, is fit for the kingdom of God." That's procrastination. A man who postpones isn't fit for the kingdom. There are a lot of people who do just that. They say, "Someday I'll give my life to Christ and serve Him, but not now." That's a dangerous attitude because they are gambling with their lives.

B. The Tragedy of Postponement

Careless people postpone for two reasons:

1. Hardened by constant rejection

The more a person resists Christ, the harder he becomes, and the easier it is to resist the next time. Man is a creature of habit.

a) Hebrews 3:7-15

Here is great proof of the inspiration of the Old Testament. The writer quotes the Old Testament, yet he attributes the quote to the Holy Spirit: "Wherefore, as the Holy Spirit saith, Today if ye will hear his voice, harden not your hearts, as in the provocation, in the day of trial in the wilderness, when your fathers put me to the test, proved me, and saw my works forty years. Wherefore, I was grieved with that generation, and said, They do always err in their heart, and they have not known my ways. So I swore in my wrath, They shall not enter into my rest" (vv. 7-11). God didn't want the Jews who were close to making a decision for Christ to be like the nation Israel. They kept hardening their hearts in the wilderness until they were prohibited from entering into the Promised Land. An entire generation died in the wilderness. Why? Because they hardened their hearts against God and forfeited rest in the Promised Land. I believe the Promised Land represented salvation to the writer of Hebrews. The nation forfeited salvation. The point of Hebrews 3:7-11 is not to do what they did.

The writer of Hebrews continues his instruction for the Jewish brethren, "Take heed, brethren, lest there be in any of you an evil heart of unbelief, in departing from the living God. But exhort one another daily, while it is called Today, lest any of you be hardened through the deceitfulness of sin" (vv. 12-13). The more you reject and the longer you put off a decision, the harder your heart becomes. Sin will deceive you into rationalizing a postponement. Verse 15 says, "While it is said, Today if ye will hear his voice, harden not your hearts."

b) Luke 13:23-25

In verse 24 Jesus says, "Strive to enter in at the narrow gate [the way of salvation]; for many, I say unto you, will seek to enter in, and shall not be able." Verse 23 indicates that few will be saved. I don't know how people can believe the doctrine of universalism and reconcile it with verses 23-24. Verse 25 says, "When once the master of the house is risen up, and hath shut the door, and ye begin to stand outside, and to knock at the door, saying, Lord, Lord, open unto us; and he shall answer and say unto you, I know you not from where ye are." There are many people who are planning on making it into heaven, but it will be too late for them—the door will be shut. They are like the people who lived in Noah's day— the door of the ark eventually was closed to them. Postponement is foolish because a person's heart can become hard.

2. Abandoned by God

After a certain time, God stops calling. In the days before Noah, God said, "My Spirit shall not always strive with man" (Gen. 6:3). Only a fool postpones salvation when his soul is at stake. He's a bigger fool than the man who put his fortune in a diamond and then accidentally dropped it into the ocean.

Review

Felix was a fool. During his tenure as procurator of Judea from A.D. 52 to 60, it was his lot to deal with Paul the apostle, even as a previous procurator by the name of Pontius Pilate had to deal with Jesus Christ. In Acts 24 Paul and Felix confront each other in a hearing. There are three ways to look at this passage: from the viewpoint of Paul and the record of what happens to him, from the viewpoint of God and how He works in the situation, or from the viewpoint of Felix and the tragedy that occurs in his life. So far we've been looking at it from Paul's viewpoint.

The Jewish leaders wanted to kill Paul because he represented a serious threat—the same threat Jesus had represented. He was winning a great following of Jews to Christ. The Jewish leaders feared that they would lose their authority in the eyes of the people. Anyone who won a great following was a threat to their position. So they tried to get rid of Paul. They tried to kill him two different times in riots

(Acts 21:27-32; 23:10) and once in an ambush (Acts 23:15). After those attempts the Romans finally decided to get Paul out of Jerusalem for two reasons: (1) Paul was a Roman citizen, so they had to protect him; and (2) he had committed no crime. The Romans took Paul to Caesarea to the home of the governor and held him in protective custody. The Jewish accusers were then called to bring their case before Felix at Caesarea. Paul would receive a much fairer trial than ever would have been possible in Jerusalem. So the accusers went to Caesarea to get Paul executed for the crimes they accused him of. The trial has three parts: the prosecution, the defense, and the verdict.

I. THE PROSECUTION (vv. 1-9; see pp. 5-15)

All the accusations brought against Paul were lies. But that's to be expected. If you live a godly life in the face of an ungodly world, you are going to suffer (2 Tim. 3:12). Paul suffered false accusations, but he could say he was blameless. God wants Christians to be called before the tribunal of the world for their faith. And He wants the verdict to be "not guilty" so that the persecution is for the sake of righteousness. If you're going to receive persecution, it ought to be the result of your holiness, not your unrighteousness.

Lesson

II. THE DEFENSE (vv. 10-21)

Paul defends himself calmly, courteously, and categorically against the charges.

A. Recognizing the Assistance (v. 10)

1. A divine lawyer (v. 10*a*)

"Then Paul, after the governor had beckoned unto him to speak, answered."

Paul didn't have a lawyer like Tertullus, who knew about Roman law and Roman courts. He had someone better than a human lawyer. When Jesus left the earth, He told His disciples that He would send them another Comforter (John 14:16). The Greek word for "Comforter" is *parakletos*. It comes from the word *para* and *kaleō*. It means "one called alongside." It could be translated "a lawyer for the defense." Paul didn't have a human lawyer, but he had the divine Lawyer handling his case. Every word Paul said to Felix was the word of the Holy Spirit—every word was inspired. Paul was doing the talking but through the energy of the Holy Spirit.

2. A competent judge (v. 10b)

"Forasmuch as I know that thou hast been of many years a judge unto this nation, I do the more cheerfully answer for myself."

Paul knew that Felix had been around long enough to judge fairly in his case, so he was anxious to answer the charges against him. Some people accuse Paul of flattery in verse 10. He didn't flatter Felix; he was just glad to have his case judged fairly. Felix had been governor in that area for five years. Prior to that, he had served under Cumanus, the governor of Samaria, for four years. So Felix had been acquainted with Jewish affairs for nine years. Any judgment rendered in regard to Jewish affairs required a prior knowledge of Jewish custom. And that custom was so unique, a man would have had to live within the culture to adequately evaluate the cultural tensions. In effect Paul is saying, "Felix, I know you've been around long enough to know that this is a theological problem. Because you know that, I'm glad to give my defense."

Is Flattery Acceptable for a Christian?

Flattery is unacceptable for a Christian at all times. When you flatter someone, you do or say something that is beyond the truth to elicit something for yourself. People don't flatter those who can't give them anything; they flatter only those who can. The things that Tertullus said about Felix were obviously not true. Tertullus knew it, Felix knew it, everyone knew it. People commonly use flattery as a way of getting what they want. And sad to say, it works. But it is absolutely unacceptable for the Christian. Why? Because Proverbs 26:28 says, "A flattering mouth worketh ruin." Psalm 12:3 says, "The Lord shall cut off all flattering lips."

What's wrong with flattery? It is not the truth. Flattery is a calculated misrepresentation to gain something for yourself. It is masked self-indulgence and selfishness—it is sin. And it is a temptation. Many people think that if you want to get anything in life, you have to get it any way you can. There are people who would say that if the church needs to build a new building, you need to flatter a person who has a lot of money. If you use that approach, you'll be waiting a long time for it.

25

I don't want money if I have to flatter someone for it. It should be fairly obvious from the way I preach that I'm not looking for money; I want people to be conformed to the image of Jesus Christ. I try not to be too rough in my preaching; I do try to admonish in love. But there's no place for flattery, even though it goes on all the time in Christian circles.

Paul was not flattering Felix. But he did know that Felix had been around long enough to make a proper judgment. For that reason he cheerfully could go ahead with his defense. I would say that there is some reverse psychology in that because it put Felix on the spot. Paul always seemed able to gain the upper hand on his opponents. Felix was pressured not only by the case but also by the fact that Paul knew he had the ability to make a responsible judgment.

B. Responding to the Accusations (vv. 11-21)

1. Sedition (vv. 11-13)

The Jewish leaders claimed Paul was a political criminal.

a) No time (v. 11)

"Because thou mayest understand, that there are yet but twelve days since I went up to Jerusalem to worship."

Paul had been in the area for only twelve days, and he spent five of them in Caesarea (Acts 24:1). The maximum time he had spent in Jerusalem was seven days. Paul is saying, "I haven't had time to start a riot." Acts 21 tells us what he was doing during those seven days.

(1) The period of the vow

When Paul arrived in Jerusalem, the Jewish Christians were concerned about Paul because they had heard he had become anti-Semitic—that he was opposed to the customs and traditions of the Jews. But Paul told them that wasn't so. The elders of the church in Jerusalem asked him to prove it by taking a Nazirite vow with four brethren. A Nazirite vow was simply an outward expression of consecration. It was a Jewish custom. Paul agreed to their request to prove he wasn't opposed to the Jewish customs. Acts

21:26-27 says, "Then Paul took the men, and the next day, purifying himself with them, entered into the temple, to signify the accomplishment of the days of purification. . . . And when the seven days were almost ended." Paul spent most of the seven days in the Temple carrying out a vow and five days in Caesarea. But the Jewish leaders accused him of starting a riot. He had been in the area for only those twelve days; there was no time to initiate any kind of a rebellion.

(2) The purpose of the vow

In Acts 24:11 Paul says, "I went up to Jerusalem to worship." He didn't go to desecrate the Temple or to start a riot but to worship. The Nazirite vow, which signified consecration, was that act of worship.

b) No riot (v. 12)

"And they neither found me in the temple disputing with any man, neither raising up the people [collecting a crowd], neither in the synagogues, nor in the city."

(1) Additional defenses

(a) Acts 25:8—This was the defense Paul gave before Festus, the governor who succeeded Felix: "Neither against the law of the Jews, neither against the temple, nor yet against Caesar, have I offended in anything at all."

(b) Acts 28:17—When Paul arrived in Rome, "it came to pass that, after three days, Paul called the chief of the Jews together; and when they were come together, he said unto them, Men and brethren, though I have committed nothing against the people or customs of our fathers, yet was I delivered prisoner." Paul had never done anything wrong. And he wasn't lying because he said he could stand before God with a clear conscience (Acts 24:16).

(2) Avoided dialogue

What did Paul deny? He said he had not been disputing in the Temple. The Greek word translated "disputing" refers to reasoning or arguing. Paul disputed in every place he traveled except Jerusalem. The Lord protected him. He did not engage in any public dialogue in the Temple. Why didn't he?

(a) Relieved of the responsibility

Paul was sensitive to the religious situation in Jerusalem—he knew it was like a powder keg. He also had been relieved of the responsibility of evangelism there, so he felt no great burden to evangelize, although I'm sure his heart was broken over Israel. He said that he had not been raising up the people (Acts 24:12). The book of Acts records that Paul reasoned out of the Scriptures in many of the cities he visited. Wherever he went, people would gather, and he would preach. But when he arrived in Jerusalem, it was time for him to pacify the Jewish Christians.

(b) Revealed by the Lord

Why would Paul not feel responsible? Why would he back away from a volatile situation? Was he afraid? No, fear was never his motive. In Acts 22:17 Paul says, "It came to pass that, when I was come again to Jerusalem [at an earlier time], even while I prayed in the temple, I was in a trance." While Paul was at another level of consciousness, God communicated to him. Acts 22:18-20 records these words of the Lord to Paul: "Make haste, and get thee quickly out of Jerusalem; for they will not receive thy testimony concerning me. And I said, Lord, they know that I imprisoned and beat in every synagoge those that believed on thee; and when the blood of thy martyr, Stephen, was shed, I also was standing by, and consenting unto his death, and kept the raiment of them that slew him." In other words, "Jerusalem would be a great place for me to preach, Lord. They would see the transformation that has taken place in me." But verse 21 says, "And he said unto me, Depart; for I will send thee far from here

28

unto the Gentiles." The Lord Jesus Christ by direct revelation told Paul that he was not responsible for the ministry in Jerusalem.

Paul's only goal in going to Jerusalem was to fellowship with Christians. He went to the Temple to carry out a vow so the Jewish Christians would not think he was anti-Semitic. He had no goal of propagating the gospel. His defenses didn't involve a specific proclamation of the gospel, although his earlier defense before the mob (Acts 22:1-21) certainly implied the truth of it. Neither did he specifically preach the gospel to the Sanhedrin. The Lord did not want him to have that particular ministry in Jerusalem. For one thing, there were already thousands of Jewish Christians there, so evangelism in Jerusalem was primarily a one-to-one encounter. People were being won to Christ. That's why Paul did not sense the drive for confrontation that he did in other places. Paul had not raised up a crowd anywhere in Jerusalem—not in the Temple or the city.

c) No proof (v. 13)

"Neither can they prove the things of which they now accuse me."

If you don't have any proof, you don't have a case. It should have been thrown out of court for that reason alone. The Jewish authorities couldn't prove anything. Paul denied the charges—he had done nothing treasonous.

2. Sectarianism (vv. 14-16)

The Jewish leaders claimed Paul was a heretic. Paul couldn't deny his Christianity, but he also had to make sure he denied their charge. So he said that he was not a heretic while at the same time he claimed to be a Christian. There was only one way he could do that: show that all his accusers were heretics.

The Way

In Acts 24:14 Paul says, "This I confess unto thee that, after the way." "The way" was a title for Christianity. Unsaved people would slur Christians by calling them Nazarenes or Christians—little Christs. But the Christians called themselves "the way." Where did that name come from? Jesus said, "I am the way" (John 14:6). Peter preached, "There is no other name under heaven given among men, whereby we must be saved" (Acts 4:12). In 2 Peter 2:2 he says, "Manyshall follow their [false teachers'] pernicious ways, by reason of whom the way of truth shall be evil spoken of."

a) Paul's clear confession (vv. 14-15)

"But this I confess unto thee that, after the way which they call heresy, so worship I the God of my fathers, believing all things which are written in the law and in the prophets; and have hope toward God, which they themselves also allow, that there shall be a resurrection of the dead, both of the just and unjust."

(1) The conflict

The topic of the resurrection would have immediately caused internal conflict with the Jewish leaders because the Sadducees didn't believe in the resurrection, whereas the Pharisees did. That's what started the fight in the Sanhedrin in Acts 23:7. Who were the real heretics? The high priests. They had ceased worshiping God because the only way to Him is through Christ. Jesus said, "No man cometh unto the Father, but by me" (John 14:6). They had ceased believing in the law and the prophets. If they still had believed, they would have had to believe in Christ because the main topic of the law and the prophets is Christ. They had also ceased believing in the great hope of Israel—the resurrection. That's a strong argument.

The Jewish leaders charged Paul with being a religious heretic who belonged to a subversive offshoot of Judaism. Paul denied it, while at the same time he affirmed that he was a Christian. He told them that Christianity was true Judaism. They were the heretics because they didn't worship the true God, believe the Scriptures, or believe in the resurrection.

Paul didn't attempt to explain any further because Felix understood the conflict between Christians and Jews. Acts 24:22 says that Felix had a "more perfect knowledge of that way," and Paul knew that he did. Felix had served in the area for nine years. Christians were everywhere. The city of Caesarea had many Christian residents, the most vocal of whom was Philip the evangelist.

(2) The convictions

(*a*) Worship of God

Paul said, "So worship I the God of my fathers" (Acts 24:14). That was a historic title for the God of Israel. Paul still worshiped the God of Israel, the God of Abraham, Isaac, and Jacob. He had not forsaken Him. That's a great truth for a Jewish Christian to make public. I think many people believe that when a Jewish person becomes a Christian, he ceases to worship the God of Israel. But He is known only through His Son. If you aren't Jewish, you might remind your family and friends that you worship the God of Israel. When one becomes a Christian, he does not forsake the God of Israel; he actually comes to Him the only way he can—through Christ.

Paul was a complete Jew. That's not a popular term today, but it's a good one. The only way a Jewish person can become all that he should be is to be made complete in Christ. In Romans 2:28-29 Paul says, "He is not a Jew who is one outwardly; neither is that circumcision which is outward in the flesh; but he is a Jew who is one inwardly; and circumcision is that of the heart." The only true Jews in the world are Christian Jews. A true Jew is one who continues to worship and obey the true God because he came to Him through the Messiah—Jesus Christ. In 1 Corinthians 16:22 Paul says, "If any man love not the Lord Jesus Christ, let him be Anathema [accursed]." In Romans 9:6 Paul says, "They are not all Israel, who are of Israel." As Paul stood before Felix, he was saying that he was the only true Jew in the trial because he had come to the Messiah.

(*b*) Belief in the law and the prophets

31

i) Paul's implication

Paul also said he believed "all things which are written in the law and in the prophets" (Acts 24:14). Do you think Paul believed the Old Testament was inspired? He believed every bit of it. But most importantly, Paul was implying that the Jewish leaders didn't, and he was right. If they had believed the law and the prophets, they would have had to believe in Christ. Today, most Jewish people have rejected Christ. That means they have also rejected the Old Testament. That's why many of them don't believe in the literal truth of the Old Testament, even though they still hold to the Judaistic ethic. But you cannot study the Old Testament very long and believe it without coming to Jesus Christ, unless you're like the ultraconservatives who are concerned only about the minutiae of the law. Most Jewish people don't even believe in a Messiah anymore; they just believe in a messianic era.

To Deny Jesus Is to Deny the Old Testament

To deny Jesus as the Messiah is to deny the Old Testament. In John 5:39 Jesus says, "Search the scriptures; for in them ye think ye have eternal life; and they are they which testify of me." On the road to Emmaus, Jesus opened up the Old Testament, and "beginning at Moses and all the prophets, he expounded unto them, in all the scriptures, the things concerning himself" (Luke 24:27). You can't study the Old Testament with an open mind and not come to Jesus Christ. To deny Jesus, a Jew must deny his own Scripture. To come to Jesus is to be complete in all that Judaism is. So Paul was saying to Felix, "I'm not a heretic. I've consummated my faith by turning to my Messiah."

It is tragic to find Jewish people all over the world who reject Jesus Christ as Messiah. By continuing to reject Him as their Messiah, they will eventually give up the idea of a Messiah. There is no one on the scene who even remotely looks like a possibility. When they don't believe He will come, they say the Messiah was an era, not a person, or they deny the possibility of a Messiah altogether. There are a few orthodox Jews who adhere to the letter of the law but who don't see Jesus as the Messiah in it.

The Saddest People

Gentile believers are better off than Jewish unbelievers. Although I have not been born into the stock of Israel and known the blessings that come as a result, I'm better off as a Gentile Christian than as an unbelieving Jew. The Bible indicates that the saddest person is an unbelieving Jew who has forfeited the truth that he had (Heb. 10:29). As a Christian who has accepted the truth, I worship the God of Israel. I believe all that the God of Israel said. And I believe in the Messiah of Israel for my salvation. I'm every bit a Jew in terms of all that I believe, if not in my nationality. I thank God that He chose to graft Gentiles into His tree (Rom. 11:17). The unbelieving branch was cut off because of its unbelief and God grafted the Gentiles in. But Christians shouldn't be smug about that, because the Bible also says that a time is coming when Israel will be grafted back in (Rom. 11:23-24). There will be a time when all Israel is saved (Rom. 11:26).

ii) Paul's identification

Paul was the only true Jew in court, while his accusers were heretics. But Paul didn't gloat over that. I imagine even as he thought about them, his heart was in pain. He loved those people. I don't believe the world can understand his love because it interprets love in such a small way. In Romans 9:1-3 Paul says, "I say the truth in Christ, I lie not, my conscience also beareth me witness in the Holy Spirit, that I have great heaviness and continual sorrow in my heart. For I could wish that I myself were accursed from Christ for my brethren, my kinsmen according to the flesh." Paul cared. In Romans 10:1 he says, "My heart's desire and prayer to God for Israel is, that they might be saved." He didn't gloat over Israel's loss; it hurt him deeply.

(c) Hope of the resurrection

According to Acts 24:15, Paul has "hope toward God." What hope? The hope of the resurrection. The traditional hope of the Jew was the resurrection. Did the Old Testament teach a resurrection? Yes, in Isaiah 26:19, Job 19:26, Daniel 12:2, and elsewhere. Abraham believed in a resurrection; that's why he was willing to sacrifice Isaac (Heb. 11:17-19). That was ultimate faith.

The Sadducees who accused Paul didn't believe in a resurrection. You might ask, "How could they avoid the teaching of the resurrection if it is in Isaiah, Job, and Daniel?" They believed that the only binding truth in the Old Testament was what Moses said (the first five books of the Old Testament). When Jesus was engaged in an argument about the resurrection with the Sadducees, He quoted Exodus 3:6 because He knew they would have to acknowledge that Scripture verse (Matt. 22:32). Jesus knew that the name of the living God—the God of Abraham, Isaac, and Jacob—indicated the reality of the resurrection. The Sadducees were not traditional; they were heretics. They denied what the Old Testament taught. I'm sure that the majority of Paul's accusers were Sadducees. The high priest was a Sadducee, as probably were the elders who accused Paul. So Paul was telling Felix that he was the only one present who believed in the resurrection of the dead, of both the just and the unjust.

b) Paul's clear conscience (v. 16)

"In this do I exercise myself, to have always a conscience void of offense toward God, and toward men."

As a true Jew—as one who believed in God, in His word, and in the hope of the resurrection—Paul wanted to live a pure life. The ultimate end of any man's testimony is his ability to say, "My desire in life is never to offend God or man." The epitome of life is to never have your conscience accuse you. Paul lived his life in accord with the standards of God. As a result, he had a clear conscience. He believed in the great truths of verses 14-15 and built his life on them. Do you know that you believe only what you act on? If you don't build your life on the principles of God, then you don't really believe them. Paul believed them and lived by them; therefore he stood blameless. Paul tried to live a life consistent with what he believed.

You ought to live a life that fits the Word of God. And you will if you truly believe it. Paul said, "I'm innocent. Just check out my life." Can you stand before the world blameless, void of offense? That's the ultimate testimony.

Focusing on the Facts

1. How did the potential follower of Jesus disqualify himself in Luke 9:57-58 (see pp. 19-20)?
2. How did the second potential follower of Jesus disqualify himself (Luke 9:59-60; see p. 20)?
3. Why do people postpone their opportunity for salvation (see pp. 21-22)?
4. Why did an entire generation of the nation of Israel forfeit their rest in the Promised Land (Heb. 3:7-11; see p. 21)?
5. Who was Paul's lawyer (see p. 23)?
6. Explain why Paul was glad to be able to give his defense before Felix (Acts 24:10; see p. 24).
7. Is flattery acceptable for a Christian? Explain (see p. 25).
8. Explain why Paul didn't have time to start a riot in Jerusalem (Acts 24:11; see p. 25).
9. Why did Paul take the Nazirite vow with four Jewish brethren (Acts 21:23-26; see p. 25)?
10. Why did Paul avoid engaging in dialogue with fellow Jews in the Temple? Explain (see pp. 26-27).
11. What was Paul's goal in going to Jerusalem in Acts 21 (see p. 28)?
12. What did the title "the way" refer to? Explain its origin (see p. 28).
13. Paul was accused of being a heretic, but who were the real heretics? Why were they heretics (see p. 29)?
14. According to Romans 2:28-29, who is a true Jew (see p. 30)?
15. When Paul said he believed "all thing which are written in the law and in the prophets," what was he implying about the Jewish leaders (Acts 24:14; see p. 31)?
16. What does a Jewish person have to deny if he denies Jesus is the Messiah (John 5:39; see p. 31)?

17. How did the Sadducees explain away the resurrection as recorded in Isaiah, Job, and Daniel? How did Jesus respond to their argument (Matt. 23:32; see p. 33)?
18. Why did Paul have a clear conscience (see p. 33)?

Pondering the Principles

1. Flattery is not acceptable for a Christian. But we are all human and fall into that worldly practice at some time. Examine your attitude toward flattery. Isolate those times when you have used flattery to gain your own end. Do you find that those occasions are frequent or infrequent? Have you flattered someone recently? Take this time to confess to God those occasions and repent of them. Memorize Ephesians 4:25: "Laying aside falsehood, speak truth, each one of you, with his neighbor, for we are members of one another" (NASB*).

2. According to Acts 24:14-15, the apostle Paul was convinced of three things: He worshiped God, believed in the law and the prophets, and hoped in the resurrection. On a scale of 1-10, evaluate your conviction of those three aspects of your Christian life. How much does your life reflect your commitment to worship God? How can the world tell that you have a deep commitment to God's Word? How do people know that you hope to be resurrected with Christ one day? Paul believed in and was committed to those great truths. As a result, he had a clear conscience before the world. You need to be building your life on those principles. Begin today to live your life with the ultimate goal of having a clear conscience before God.

*New American Standard Bible.

3
Paul's Trial Before Felix—Part 3
The Tragedy of Postponing Salvation

Outline

Review
I. The Prosecution (vv. 1-9)
II. The Defense (vv. 10-21)
   A. Recognizing the Assistance (v. 10)
   B. Responding to the Accusations (vv. 11-21)
      1. Sedition (vv. 11-13)
      2. Sectarianism (vv. 14-16)

Lesson
      3. Sacrilege (vv. 17-21)
        a) Paul's reason for coming to Jerusalem (v. 17)
        b) Paul's reiteration of his innocence (v. 18)
        c) Paul's requests to Felix (vv. 19-20)
          (1) Present eyewitnesses to the crime (v. 19)
          (2) Present a report from the council (v. 20)
        d) Paul's redirection of the issue (v. 21)
III. The Verdict (vv. 22-27)
   A. Postponing the case (vv. 22-23)
      1. Felix's incredible cowardice (v. 22)
        a) His information (v. 22*a*)
        b) His indecision (v. 22*b*)
      2. Paul's partial confinement (v. 23)
   B. Postponing Salvation (vv. 24-27)
      1. The request (v. 24*a*)
      2. The revelation (vv. 24*b*-25*a*)
        a) The content of the gospel (v. 24*b*)
        b) The character of the gospel (v. 25*a*)
          (1) Conviction presented
            (*a*) Righteousness
            (*b*) Self-control
            (*c*) Judgment
          (2) Conviction perceived

3. The resistance (vv. 25*b*-27)
    a) The decision of a fool (v. 25*b*)
    b) The desire of a fool (v. 26*a*)
    c) The delay of a fool (v. 26*b*)
    d) The defeat of a fool (v. 27)

Review

Acts 24:1-27 is about the tragedy of a man who had a great opportunity for salvation but postponed it. His name was Felix, and he was the Roman governor assigned to Judea. The apostle Paul was on trial before him. Paul had been accused of certain crimes, all of them false. The charges had been drummed up by some antagonistic Jewish leaders who wanted to see Paul dead because he was a threat to their theological security. The case eventually found its way to Felix. As we examine the case, we not only see Paul exhibiting his blameless life but God working as well. Particularly in this lesson we see Felix, a tragic man who squandered his opportunity for eternal life.

Felix had to make a judgment in the case of Paul. The problem that began in Jerusalem when the Jewish leaders tried to kill Paul was pushed to a higher court—the court of Felix in Caesarea, the Roman headquarters. Beyond the legal decision that Felix had to make regarding Paul, he had to make a personal decision regarding Jesus Christ. And the record that remains is of a man who forfeited a tremendous opportunity. Few men have had the privilege of having the apostle Paul in their house for two years. Yet despite all that Felix was exposed to, he rejected salvation.

I. THE PROSECUTION (vv. 1-9; see pp. 5-15, 23)

Christians Should Expect False Charges

Paul expected false charges. I think that Christians who live holy lives in Satan's world will always have to contend with false accusations. To see this perspective, let's look at a prophecy and a statement that Jesus made.

1. Matthew 10:16-39

    a) The expectations

    When Jesus sent out His disciples, He told them to anticipate certain problems and how to react to them.

    (1) Hostility

    Matthew 10:16 says, "Behold, I send you forth as sheep in the midst of wolves." The first thing He says indicates that they would face a certain amount of hostility when they began to confront the world with the truth. Then He said, "Be ye, therefore, wise as serpents" (v. 16). They needed to be shrewd and careful in planning their strategy. They also needed to be as "harmless [innocent] as doves." Paul continually revealed his blamelessness and his cleverness in the way he was able to construct an opportunity to present the gospel in the midst of a hostile audience.

(2) Evil men

Matthew 10:17 says, "Beware of men." The disciples' biggest problem would be people. He didn't say, "Beware of Satan," because it is assumed that Satan is behind the scene. Jesus continues, "For they will deliver you up to the councils, and they will scourge you in their synagogues, and ye shall be brought before governors and kings for my sake, for a testimony against them and the Gentiles" (vv. 17-18). Jesus instructed them not to naively trust others and become sucked into their confidence, fall into their traps, or to do anything that would enable them to bring a valid charge against them. Paul had already experienced being brought into the councils of men. He was on the verge of being scourged in Fort Antonia, saved only by the fact of his Roman citizenship. In Acts 24 Paul is brought before the governor, Felix, and in Acts 26 he is brought before a king, Agrippa. Paul fulfilled Jesus' prophecy in Matthew 10:17, and it was fulfilled by all the apostles to some extent.

(3) Divine inspiration

Jesus gave some comforting words in the midst of His warnings: "But when they deliver you up, be not anxious how or what ye shall speak; for it shall be given you in that same hour what ye shall speak. For it is not ye that speak, but the Spirit of your Father who speaketh in you" (vv. 19-20). That was a direct promise to the apostles; I don't believe Christians can expect that today. The promise of divine inspiration belonged only to the apostles. In John 14:26 Jesus says, "The Holy Spirit, whom the Father will send in my name, he shall teach you all things, and bring all things to your remembrance, whatever I have said unto you." The Holy Spirit would give the gospel writers accurate recall of all that Jesus said. When the apostles opened their mouths, the Spirit would speak through them. The Holy Spirit does lead and guide us, but God doesn't talk through us as He did through the apostles and writers of Scripture. Paul received inspiration in all six phases of his trial. God gave him the words, and they are recorded in the Word of God.

(4) Family strife

Matthew 10:21 says, "The brother shall deliver up the brother to death, and the father the child; and the children shall rise up against their parents, and cause them to be put to death."

b) The explanation

Matthew 10:22 says, "Ye shall be hated of all men for my name's sake." The reason for the hostility is Jesus Christ. First John 5:19 says, "The whole world lieth in [the lap of] wickedness." Since Satan controls the world and hates Christ, the system that persecutes the believer is really persecuting Christ. Christians will suffer for Christ's sake because of who He is and the world's hatred of Him.

c) The encouragement

Matthew 10:26 says, "Fear them not, therefore; for there is nothing covered that shall not be revealed; and hidden, that shall not be known." In other words, "Don't be afraid because there will come a time when judgment will be accomplished and proper rewards will be given. The true and the false will be unmasked." Verses 27-28 say, "What I tell you in darkness, that speak in light; and what ye hear in the ear [in secret], that proclaim upon the housetops. And fear not them who kill the body, but are not able to kill the soul; but rather fear him who is able to destroy both soul and body in hell." Fear God, not men. If you fear men, then you don't give a bold testimony. But fearing God will cause you to open your mouth, because you'll want to be obedient to Him.

God knows all about you. Jesus said, "Are not two sparrows sold for a farthing? And one of them shall not fall on the ground without your Father [knowing]. But the very hairs of your head are all numbered. Fear not, therefore; ye are of more value than many sparrows" (vv.

29-31). We should expect persecution, but God will care for us, so we shouldn't be afraid of it.

We need to be willing to pay a price. And the price is animosity from the system. In verses 36-39 Jesus says, "A man's foes shall be they of his own household. He that loveth father or mother more than me, is not worthy of me. . . . And he that taketh not his cross and followeth after me, is not worthy of me. He that findeth his life shall lose it." There is a price to be paid: Expect false charges. And you will be accused because the world still hates Christ. Satan hates Christ, and he attacks Him through those who name the name of Christ.

2. Luke 6:22-23

Jesus said, "Blessed are ye, when men shall hate you, and when they shall separate you from their company" (v. 22). Has that ever happened to you? When someone finds out you're a Christian, does he avoid having anything to do with you? That is alienation. Jesus added that people will "reproach you [criticize you], and cast out your name as evil" (v. 22). But when all that happens, you are blessed "for the Son of man's sake" (v. 22). What should be your reaction when they do that? Verse 23 says, "Rejoice ye in that day, and leap for joy; for, behold, your reward is great in heaven." You need to expect that the world is going to be antagonistic, so you should expect false charges. They didn't come as a shock to Paul.

II. THE DEFENSE (vv. 10-21)

Having heard the false charges, Paul answers them when asked to do so by Felix in verse 10.

A. Recognizing the Assistance (v. 10; see pp. 23-25)

B. Responding to the Accusations (vv. 11-21)

1. Sedition (vv. 11-13; see pp. 25-28)

The Reversed Perspective

As we consider the Jewish leaders' accusations of Paul, I see an illustration of man's inability to make a sound evaluation. Felix was evil, immoral, materialistic, and oppressive. He ruled with brutality and gained his position by collusion and corruption. The apostle Paul was gentle, godly, Spirit-filled, courageous, selfless, truthful, and hard-working. But what did the Jewish leaders say?

"Most noble Felix" (v. 3). The world's perspective is the reverse of the godly one. The contrast between Paul and Felix reminds one of Jesus and Barabbas. The lovely Son of God and a common, ordinary criminal were presented to the people so that one could be set free. The people said, "Not this man, but Barabbas" (John 18:40). One of the sins that destroyed Israel was the exaltation of evil men (Mal. 3:15). Paul was accused. But the ones who should have been accused for their corruption were Felix and the Jewish leaders.

2. Sectarianism (vv. 14-16; see pp. 28-34)

Lesson

3. Sacrilege (vv. 17-21)

The Jewish leaders also accused Paul of attempting to profane the sacred Temple, which was to claim he was blaspheming God.

a) Paul's reason for coming to Jerusalem (v. 17)

"After many years I came to bring alms to my nation, and offerings."

Paul's motive in going to Jerusalem was not to blaspheme God. After many years (four years since his last visit or even longer since he actually had lived there), he came simply to bring alms to his nation. "Alms" refers to the money he had brought for the needy. He had collected that money from Gentile Christians to offer to the Jewish Christians as a sign of love. Paul also said that he brought offerings in addition to alms. What's the difference between alms and offerings? "Alms" is the definition of what he brought—the gift of money; "offerings" is the bringing of that gift. The alms were a gift to the needy from the Gentiles.

Paul said he came to bring alms to his "nation." But he didn't give the alms to the nation; he gave them to the Christian Jews. Remember that the only true Jew is a Christian Jew—one who is a Jew inwardly, not outwardly (Rom. 2:28-29). Paul didn't distinguish the Christian Jew from the nation because in his mind a true Jew was one who believed in the Messiah, Jesus Christ. In that sense he brought alms to his nation.

42

b) Paul's reiteration of his innocence (v. 18)

"Whereupon certain Jews from Asia [Asia Minor, a Roman province that included Ephesus, a city where Paul had preached for three years] found me purified in the temple, neither with multitude, nor with tumult."

Paul was in the Temple carrying out the purification rites for a Nazirite vow and worshiping in the customary manner. When the Jews from Asia Minor found him there, no multitude was gathered, and no riot was taking place. He was doing nothing illegal. He had not desecrated the Temple, and no multitude had accused him of it while he was there. If Paul had brought a Gentile into the inner part of the Temple, a riot would have occurred. But there was no tumult and no crowd. Paul was simply carrying out his vow when the Jews from Asia seized him.

The Jews saw an opportunity to get rid of Paul, so they raised up a mob and tried to kill him (Acts 21:27-30). They were angry with him because many Jews had been saved in their own province. That put a dent in their synagogue attendance and undermined their operation. But Paul testified that there wasn't a crowd and that he hadn't violated anything. Rather than desecrating the Temple, he was purifying himself. He had just gone through a time of dedication and commitment that was far from desecration.

c) Paul's requests to Felix (vv. 19-20)

(1) Present eyewitnesses to the crime (v. 19)

"Who ought to have been here before thee, and object, if they had anything against me."

Paul is saying that if a riot had occurred, some of the people who were in it should be giving testimony to it. He is asking the Jewish leaders, "Where are your witnesses? You say I was desecrating the Temple, but who says so? Where are the eyewitnesses who saw me take a Gentile into the inner court of the Temple?" There weren't any, because he hadn't done it. And they may have been afraid to bring in a false witness because they wouldn't want his lie to be exposed.

(2) Present a report from the council (v. 20)

"Or else let these same here [Ananias and the elders] say, if they have found any evil doing in me, while I stood before the council."

Paul was saying, "If there are no eyewitnesses of the supposed desecration of the Temple, why don't you let the Jewish leaders tell you what they determined in their council?" The council did meet, but the meeting ended in a riot, and they didn't find out anything (Acts 23:1-10). So the Jewish leaders had nothing to say.

There was no accusation from witnesses and none from the Jewish hearing. They could only accuse Paul of one thing, which Paul brings up in verse 21.

d) Paul's redirection of the issue (v. 21)

"Except it be for this one thing, that I cried standing among them, Concerning the resurrection of the dead I am called in question by you this day."

The only thing Paul could be accused of is making an issue out of the resurrection. And Paul knew that was not a criminal issue but a theological one. Theological issues were not decided by courts. Incidentally, Felix also knew it wasn't an issue for the court. In Acts 23:29 he receives a letter from Claudius Lysias, the tribune of Jerusalem, who explains, "I perceived [Paul] to be accused of questions of their law, but to have nothing laid to his charge worthy of death or of bonds." Claudius knew that Paul hadn't done anything to break the law but that the Jewish leaders were upset over a theological issue.

Paul ended his testimony by throwing the case into the area of theology. That was a wise move. Paul knew from experience that a Roman judge could not make a determination in a case regarding Jewish theology. There was no crime with which to try Paul. Felix knew the real issue, and Paul passed to him the responsibility of making the right decision.

The key to Paul's testimony is in verse 16, "In this do I exercise myself, to have always a conscience void of offense toward God, and toward men." Paul had a clear conscience—his life was blameless. It is a tremendous thing to be able to stand in front of a court and not only be as wise as a serpent but also be as blameless and innocent as a dove. And when you rebuke all those who would accuse you by your pure life and words, you put to silence their accusations.

III. THE VERDICT (vv. 22-27)

What is the only appropriate verdict that could be rendered? Innocent. There weren't any witnesses. The preliminary hearing held by the Sanhedrin came up with no conclusion. The only issue that was involved in the case was theological. So what verdict does Felix give in the case? He was a competent man who had judged cases before. He knew that the Jewish leaders perjured themselves throughout the trial. When they first arrived, Tertullus flattered Felix with lies. They lied about what happened when Claudius Lysias rescued Paul. Felix already knew what went on from the letter he received from Claudius. They also lied about the accusations because they had no witnesses to support them. They lied about everything. When Paul finished his defense, they didn't have anything to say. But Felix had a problem. He knew the leaders had lied, but he was afraid. What was he afraid of? For one thing, he was trying a Roman citizen, and a Roman citizen had certain rights. If those rights were not met, Paul could make trouble for Felix. But he had an even worse problem: There were many angry Jews in his court— and angry Jews had been known to start revolutions in the past. A governor who was having trouble with revolutions was in worse trouble with Rome.

Pontius Pilate had a similar problem. He ultimately allowed Jesus to be crucified to pacify the Jewish leaders because he was afraid he would lose his job if he didn't rule well. Felix was trapped in the same way. His relationship to Rome and its laws was at stake, but so was his relationship to the Jewish leaders. So he did what many politicians do: nothing. He compromised. I'm not saying all people in public office do that, but I am saying that many do.

A. Postponing the case (vv. 22-23)

    1. Felix's incredible cowardice (v. 22)

        a) His information (v. 22*a*)

        "And when Felix heard these things, having more perfect knowledge of that way."

        What was "that way"? Christianity; Felix had more perfect knowledge of Christianity than Paul's Jewish accusers did. He was an informed man. Now why did the Holy Spirit include that in verse 22? It gives us some added insight into how responsible Felix was to make a right judgment. He knew enough about Christianity to do what was right. He also knew that the case was based on a theological debate between Judaism and Christianity. Luke (the writer of the book of Acts) is telling us that Felix knew what he should have done.

b) His indecision (v. 22b)

"He deferred them, and said, When Lysias, the chief captain, shall come down, I will determine your case."

There is no record that he ever called Claudius Lysias or that he ever came. Felix postponed the case permanently. That was the act of a coward.

You might be wondering how Felix had a knowledge of Christianity. He lived in Caesarea. Philip the evangelist lived there, as did many Christians. Felix also spent nine years in Judea, and tens of thousands of Christians lived throughout Judea. So he knew enough to evaluate correctly that this case was theological in nature, not criminal. He knew enough about Christianity to be responsible. But he was like Pilate—convinced of the testimony of the accused but afraid of the Jewish leaders. So he postponed the decision until Claudius Lysias could add some information, but Felix never called him. It was a convenient non-decision.

2. Paul's partial confinement (v. 23)

"He commanded a centurion [a soldier who commanded one hundred men] to keep Paul, and let him have liberty, and that he should forbid none of his acquaintances to minister or come unto him."

Felix decided to put Paul into a partial confinement to pacify his conscience. Paul was under the care of a centurion, but he had liberty, and his friends and acquaintances could visit him at will.

At this point the story of Paul's trial before Felix ends. What I see in those twenty-three verses is the innocence of Paul. His character was blameless. Acts 24:1-23 is the record of an innocent man brought before a pagan judge by Jewish accusers. Paul's case was like that of Christ: If there had been any true accusation, it would have been made. If there were any bona fide witnesses who saw the crime, they would have testified at the trial. But there were no true accusations and no bona fide witnesses. If there had been one small blemish in Paul's life, his accusers would have had a witness ready to accuse him of it. But the Jewish leaders had no such witness and therefore had nothing to say. Paul was as wise as a serpent and as harmless as a dove. He was innocent. If you live your life for Jesus Christ and are accused of something, you should be able to stand against those accusations with a conscience like Paul's—innocent, blameless, and holy. This trial gives us a beautiful picture of a holy man who could stand before a group of people who searched for any conceivable accusation, yet could find nothing. It should be the same in your life.

Why Did God Allow Paul to Remain a Prisoner?

How do we see God in Acts 24? Verse 27 says that Paul remained imprisoned for two years. Was God's plan overruled? Did God have to wait to act while Paul sat in jail? Was the plan of God interrupted? No. Was Paul's imprisonment in the sovereign will of God? If it was, why did He allow it? Some people think Paul needed the time to plan his strategy for Rome, but I'm not sure that's true. After all, he remained a prisoner in Rome, and there isn't much strategy involved in that. Other people say he needed to become accustomed to the Roman style of living. But Paul was already accustomed to that. He had traveled in Roman countries for years. If those reasons aren't true, then why did the Lord want Paul to remain a prisoner in Caesarea for two years?

During those two years we have no record of any sermon Paul preached or of anything he wrote. Can you imagine the apostle Paul not preaching or writing for two years? He may have preached or written something, but we don't have any record of it. I think those two years may have been a furlough—he needed a rest. He had accomplished much in a few years. He had journeyed all over the Roman world. Those travels climaxed with his arrival in Jerusalem. First, he was nearly beaten to death. Next he was thrown into custody and hustled to Caesarea by 470 Roman soldiers. Then he had to endure a mock trial. I think he finally reached the place in his service for the Lord where he had to stop for a while.

One key thought from Acts 24:23 leads me to think that Paul needed rest: "He commanded a centurion to keep Paul, and to let him have liberty, and that he should forbid none of his acquaintances to minister." The implication is that Paul needed to be ministered to. I believe that Luke and Aristarchus were with Paul. Philip probably came around quite often. There probably were many believers in the area of Caesarea who spent some time with him during those two years. I'm sure he discipled some people. I also think that we will find some of Felix's soldiers when we get to heaven. Perhaps the centurion of verse 23 is there. So I think the two-year imprisonment was a time when God let Paul rest from what he had endured in preparaton for the worst still to come, his eventual execution. We can be sure of one thing: God knows all. God knew that Paul needed two years in Caesarea. And whatever God accomplished, He accomplished within His purpose—not outside of it.

B. Postponing Salvation (vv. 24-27)

Felix is a sad character. His past was bad, his present was filled with compromise and indecision, and his future became tragic.

1. The request (v. 24a)

   "After certain days, when Felix came with his wife, Drusilla, who was a Jewess, he sent for Paul."

   Felix may have had his exposure to Christianity from Drusilla. Drusilla was the daughter of Herod Agrippa I, the Herod named in Acts 12, who would have been familiar with the beginnings of Christianity. She may have been inquisitive about all the facts of Christianity, as was Felix. Incidentally, Felix first saw her when she was married to the king of Emesa, which was part of Syria, when she was around fifteen. Accordintg to the historians, she was supposed to be a raving beauty. Felix eventually seduced her and stole her from her husband. Their relationship was immoral from the beginning.

2. The revelation (vv. 24b-25a)

   a) The content of the gospel (v.24b)

      "[Felix] heard him concerning the faith in Christ."

      The verse says, "concerning *the* faith," not just "faith" (emphasis added). Paul didn't speak concerning putting one's faith in Christ but concerning the faith in Christ. Faith in Christ is subjective; the faith is objective. Paul gave them the content of the gospel. He told Felix that Jesus is God. He told him that Jesus was born of a virgin and lived a miraculous life. He told him that Jesus died on the cross for the deliverance of sin and rose the third day from the dead. Paul told him all the facts of the gospel. That's what Jude was referring to when he said, "Contend for the faith" (Jude 3). The content of the gospel is the embodiment of truth. Paul talked about who Chrsit was, why He came, and what He accomplished while Felix and Drusilla listened.

b) The character of the gospel (v. 25*a*)

"And as he reasoned of righteousness, self-control, and judgment to come, Felix trembled."

(1) Conviction presented

Important parts of the Christian faith are righteousness, self-control, and judgment. Those three areas must be included in the presentation of the gospel.

(*a*) Righteousness—This is God's divine ideal—His absolute standard. What does God demand? Absolute righteousness. Jesus said, "Be ye, therefore, perfect, even as your Father, who is in heaven, is perfect" (Matt. 5:48). God's absolute demand is righteousness.

(*b*) Self-control—This is man's required response. God has an absolute ideal, and you have to control yourself to conform to that standard. Paul presented Felix with God's standard and showed him that God demands conformity to it.

(*c*) Judgment—When man doesn't conform to God's standard, judgment will come. Man must conform to God's absolute ideal or be judged.

After Paul presented the ideal of righteousness, he exposed Felix's lack of self-control. Sitting next to him was the woman he had seduced and stolen. Paul talked to Felix about his sin and the fact that he had not lived up to God's standard of absolute righteousness. Felix lived far below that standard. His ultimate end was judgment.

The gospel must be presented so that it convicts those who hear it. Verses 24-25 give us a pattern for evangelism. There are two sides: (1) the problem of sin, righteousness, self-control, and judgment; and (2) the faith in Christ—who He was and what He did to overcome man's inability to meet God's standard. The gospel is simply this: Tell a man what God's standard is, show him that he is not living up to it, and tell him that he will be judged if he doesn't live up to it. Then tell him that since he can't live up to it, Jesus Christ took his sin, paid his penalty of judgment, and offers him His righteousness by faith.

John 16:8 says that the Holy Spirit has come to convict men of sin, righteousness, and judgment. Righteousness is God's absolute ideal, sin is man's inability to live up to it, and judgment is the result if he doesn't. If you present righteousness, sin, and judgment, you are following the path of the Spirit. You have to present the gospel by covering those three truths because the Spirit wants to convict men of them.

  (2) Conviction perceived

    Felix was convicted. Acts 24:25 says that he trembled. The Greek word indicates that he shuddered. When the apostle Paul presented the facts of the gospel, the Holy Spirit used them to convict Felix, so much so that he began to shake and tremble.

 3. The resistance (vv. 25*b*-27)

  a) The decision of a fool (v. 25*b*)

    "And [Felix] answered, Go thy way for this time; when I have a convenient season, I will call for thee."

    As long as Felix was shaking from conviction, he still was open to the gospel. But it wasn't long before he stopped trembling, and when he heard Paul, it didn't mean a thing to him. A habit that starts out as small as a thread that a child can break soon becomes a cord that a giant can't sever. When someone continues to resist, it becomes harder and harder for him to change. That's why Paul told the Corinthians, "Now is the day of savlation" (2 Cor. 6:2).

    W. Clarkson said, "If vice has slain its thousands, and pride its thousands, surely procrastination has slain its tens of thousands. The man who is consciously refusing to serve God knows where he stands and what he is; he knows that he is a rebel against God, standing on perilous ground. But he who thinks he is about to enter the kingdom, shelters himself under the cover of his imaginary submission and goes on and on until sinful habit has him in its iron chain, or until pale faced Death knocks at his door, and he is found unready." He's right. It is better for a man to be hostile against the gospel than it is for a man to hang on the edge of salvation but never come. The deceitfulness of sin fools him into thinking he will eventually do what he won't do. Now is the time of salvation, but the foolish man procrastinates.

Archias, a supreme magistrate of Thebes, was celebrating at a feast when a courier ran in great haste to present him with important letters. Archias said, "Tomorrow," and he laughed and stuffed the letter under his couch. That same night conspirators attacked and slaughtered everyone in the palace. As long as Felix continued to tremble there was hope, but when he quit trembling he was in trouble.

b) The desire of a fool (v. 26*a*)

"He hoped also that money should have been given him of Paul, that he might loose him."

Felix wanted a bribe out of Paul. He was so materialistic that he would do for money what he wouldn't do for justice. He would allow himself to be put in jeopardy for money but nothing else. He wasn't about to let Paul go because the Jewish leaders might give him trouble. But he might have let Paul go if he got money, and then he wouldn't care if they troubled him. Paul told Timothy, "The love of money is the root of all evil" (1 Tim. 6:10). And Felix loved money.

What would make Felix think Paul had money? He probably thought that since Paul brought a lot of money to Jerusalem and since he was the leader of the Nazarenes, he might have some money on hand. Or he might have thought the Christians could have pooled their money and bought him off.

c)   The delay of a fool (v. 26*b*)

"Wherefore, he sent for him the oftener, and communed with him."

Felix sent for Paul again and again. What do you think Paul talked about? The gospel, of course. But the sad part is, Scripture doesn't record that Felix was ever convicted again. There never was a convenient season. He just wanted money. Jesus said, "What shall it profit a man, if he shall gain the whole world, and lose his soul? Or what shall a man give in exchange for his soul?" (Mark 8:36-37). What price would Felix pay for his soul?

d)   The defeat of a fool (v. 27)

"But after two years Porcius Festus came into Felix's place; and Felix, willing to show the Jews a favor, left Paul bound."

Felix was removed from his governorship when there was a big riot in Caesarea. He put it down with such violence that the Jews were outraged and managed to obtain his recall from Rome. But he was afraid that the Jews would pursue him even when he was out of office. He had already lost his job, and he was afraid he might lose his life. So he attempted to pacify the Jewish leaders by leaving Paul a prisoner. For two years Paul had to remain a prisoner. The case was never closed, and a final testimony was never given.

Felix was a man who preserved his position, a man who wanted money but who forfeited what mattered. He became a classic illustration of one who has all the necessary information. Hebrews 10:26-27 says of such a man, "If we sin willfully after we have received the knowledge of the truth, there remaineth no more sacrifice for sins, but a certain fearful looking for of judgment." Shakespeare put it this way in *Julius Caesar* (IV.iii.209):

There is a tide in the affairs of men,
Which taken at the flood, leads on to fortune;
Omitted, all the voyage of their life
Is bound in shallows and in miseries.
On such a full sea we are now afloat,
And we must take the current when it serves,
Or lose.

Shakespeare was right. Felix lost. I'm sure that some of you have thought about receiving Jesus Christ, but you've never done it. You've said to yourself, "Someday I'm going to receive Him—someday when there is a convenient season." There has never been a convenient season. You are being deceived by sin to think that there ever will be. Don't harden your heart. Come while you still have the opportunity to receive Christ.

Focusing on the Facts

1. What should Christians expect when they live holy lives in Satan's world (see p. 37)?
2. Why did Jesus tell the disciples that they needed to beware of men (Matt. 10:17; see p. 38)?
3. Explain how Paul fulfilled Jesus' prophecy of Matthew 10:17 (see p. 38).
4. Why are Christians hated by the world (Matt. 10:22; see p. 39)?
5. What happens when believers fear men? What happens when they fear God (see pp. 39-40)?
6. How should believers react when they are alienated for being Christians (Luke 6:23; see p. 40)?
7. What was Paul's motive for going to Jerusalem (Acts 24:17; see p. 41)?
8. Why did the Jews from Asia Minor want to kill Paul (see p. 42)?
9. According to Acts 24:19-20, what did Paul ask Felix to present (see pp. 42-43)?
10. What was the only accusation that the Jewish leaders could raise against Paul? Why did Paul report that to Felix (see p. 43)?
11. What was the only appropriate verdict for a case like Paul's? Why (see p. 44)?
12. What was the major problem Felix faced in pronouncing the verdict in Paul's case (see p. 44)?
13. Why did Felix have the insight to make a right decision in Paul's case? What decision did he make (Acts 24:22; see p. 45)?
14. Describe Paul's confinement in Caesarea (Acts 24:23; see pp. 45-46).
15. Give some possible reasons for God's allowing Paul to remain in confinement for two years (see pp. 46-47).
16. What is the faith in Christ that Paul shared with Felix (see p. 48)?
17. What were the three things Paul talked about that caused Felix to tremble? Explain each one. Why did Felix tremble (Acts 24:25; see pp. 48-49)?

18. What pattern does Acts 24:24-25 provide for believers? Explain (see p. 49).
19. What was Felix willing to do for money that he wouldn't do for justice (Acts 24:26; see p. 50)?
20. Why did Felix leave Paul in confinement when he was removed from his post as governor (Acts 24:27; see p. 51)?

Pondering the Principles

1. In Matthew 10:16 Jesus instructs the disciples to be as wise as serpents. That instruction needs to be heeded by all believers today—especially by those who confront unbelievers with God's truth. One of the best ways Christians can begin to learn practical wisdom is to read the book of Proverbs. If you commit yourself to read one chapter a day, you will finish the book in a month. Then read it again the next month, and the next one. The majority of the Proverbs were written by Solomon, who prayed for wisdom and was made the wisest man on earth by God (1 Kings 3:11-12). But Jesus also told the disciples to be as innocent as doves. Wisdom must be balanced with a blameless life. Despite all his wisdom, Solomon turned from God and worshiped the idols of his many wives. As you read Proverbs and follow the Lord's instruction, ask God to continually remind you of the importance of living a blameless life.

2. Whom do you fear most: God or men? Why? Be honest in your answer. Most of us, at one time or another, have feared men more than we feared God. How was your witness for Christ affected by that fear? If you presently fear God more than men, does your witness for Christ to the unsaved reflect that fear? If it doesn't, you may need to more honestly evaluate your fear of God. Ask God to search your heart and reveal your attitude toward Him. Confess to Him any sin that has put men and the things of this world before Him. Ask God to instill in you a reverence for Him and the proper perspective of man's relationship to Him.

3. Acts 24:24-25 gives us a good pattern to follow when we share the gospel with people. What was the content of the gospel Paul shared with Felix? What are the three key elements about sin that Paul shared with Felix and that we need to share as well? Write those things on a piece of paper and keep it in your Bible. As you study God's Word, add verses to that list that can help you in your presentation of the gospel. For example, Matthew 5:48 is a

good verse to share with people about God's standard of righteousness. Remember, you need to "be ready always to give an answer to every man that asketh you a reason of the hope that is in you, with meekness and fear" (1 Pet. 3:15).

4
Paul Before Festus—Part 1

Outline

Introduction
A. The Position
B. The Phases
C. The Principles

Lesson   ˈ
I. The Assassination Plotted (vv. 1-5)
   A. The Unfortunate Legacy (v. 1)
      1. The ascension
      2. The animosity
         a) Against Pilate
         b) Against Felix
         c) Against Antiochus Epiphanes
   B. The Unwise Leadership (vv. 2-3)
      1. The request motivated by their hatred
      2. The reasons motivating their hatred
         a) The hatred of religious people toward Christianity
            (1) The origin of false religion
            (2) The origin of false doctrine
               (*a*) John 15:18-25
               (*b*) John 16:9
            (3) The origin of false teachers
         b) The power of a blameless life
         c) The power of sin
   C. The Unforeseen Limitation (vv. 4-5)
      1. The proposal
      2. The plan
         a) The providence of God
         b) The place of defense
II. The Accusation Presented (vv. 6-7)
   A. The Accusations
      1. Sedition
      2. Sectarianism

3. Sacrilege

B. The Application

Introduction

A. The Position

Acts 25 describes the life of the apostle Paul as a prisoner. He was a prisoner first in Jerusalem, then in Caesarea, and finally in Rome, where tradition suggests he was executed. Paul had completed the missionary journeys spoken of in the biblical account, although there may have been a period of time after Paul's initial imprisonment in Rome where he was able to do some missionary work, possibly in Spain.

The Holy Spirit has chosen to detail in great length the trials and defenses of the apostle Paul. But one cannot help wondering why Acts 21-28 is so heavily saturated with the defenses Paul made before the various judgment seats of men.

There is a noticeable lack of any doctrine in this section of Scripture, although there is some at the end of Acts 28 in verses 23-31. There is no great cataclysmic salvation story, no church founded, nor any great missionary enterprise embarked upon. There is only one allusion to the gospel in Acts 25:19. Acts 21-28 is written in historical, narrative style characteristic of the book of Acts. In studying this passage, I asked myself, "Why is God here detailing accusations, court procedures, and defenses as opposed to doctrinal issues?" Then I realized that Paul had faced a strategic point in his life.

B. The Phases

1. The mob in Jerusalem

The mob in Jerusalem tried to kill Paul, so the Romans rescued him and allowed him to give his first defense to the Jewish crowd that tried to kill him (Acts 22).

2. The mayhem in the Sanhedrin

The Romans didn't know what to do with Paul, so they decided to try him in front of the Sanhedrin, which was the Jewish high court. Paul gave his second defense to the Sanhedrin and left them in chaos, arguing with each other (Acts 23:6-7).

3. The meeting in Caesarea

The Romans decided that Paul should be taken to Caesarea and tried before Felix, who was then governor of the Roman province of Judea. Paul was given an opportunity to bring the third phase of his defense (Acts 24).

4. The matter before Festus

We have already seen accusations against Paul three times, and yet the Holy Spirit describes the same accusations in chapter 25 as Paul is being led before Festus, the new governor who replaces Felix.

5. The message before Agrippa

Paul also gave his defense before King Herod Agrippa II (Acts 26). Throughout the narrative of Acts 21-28, Paul is defending himself in the various trials against him.

C. The Principles

As you look at this portion of the book of Acts, you might be confused about the intent of the Holy Spirit. If you read this portion of Scripture casually, you would miss the underlying principles, because the good part is hidden underneath the surface. We are going to study some profound principles underneath the surface of this passage. The text isn't any less important just because the illustration is on the top and the truth underneath. What are the principles in Acts 25:1-12?

1. The power of a blameless life

One of the things we see again and again in the life of the apostle Paul is that each time he was tried before a human court, he was always rendered innocent. The best courts in the world acquitted him of any crime. That shows the tremendous power of a blameless Christian testimony. The Jewish leaders tried to convict him of wrongdoing but could not find one thing to accuse him of. His innocence stood as a temendous rebuke of their own sin.

2. The hatred of religious people toward Christianity

It is amazing that the most volatile hostility in the world toward Christianity comes from religious people. The reason is that Satan is the master of all religion. Satan is fighting against God and Christ and is the one who developed all systems of religion outside of Christianity. All counterfeit religious systems are spawned by Satan, who disguises himself as an angel of light (2 Cor. 11:14). All false religions fight the truth.

Historically, the greatest persecutors of Christianity have been religious people. Don't expect religious people to be tolerant of Christianity. Satan is the head of all false religion and is absolutely intolerant toward Christ and Christianity.

3. The power of sin

When someone habitually sins, he becomes a captive to his sin. The habit is almost unbreakable. That is what Paul meant when he talked about being a slave to sin (Rom. 6:17).

4. The pattern of persecution from the world

Spirit-filled, effective Christians always create problems in the world. That is why the world persecutes Christianity. When a person lives a godly life, it shows the world its sin.

5. The courage of a committed Christian

One of the lost virtues for many Christians is courage, which is the external reality of an internal faith. Courage is the legitimizing of my faith, because if I really believe God, I will step out in faith. Courage is the response to faith. Paul showed unbelievable courage because he believed God.

6. The exoneration of Christianity

True Christianity forever stands innocent in the face of an accusing world. One of the early criticisms of Christianity was that it was attempting to overthrow the existing governments. That is why, in the book of Acts, the Holy Spirit records the trials of Christians before the Roman world to show that they are innocent and law abiding. That is important for the world to know. Unfortunately, some of Christendom through the centuries has become largely political, as it is in Ireland today, and is a defamation of the Lord Jesus Christ Himself.

7. The impact of the totally committed life

Many have wondered what one man alone could possibly do to affect the world. But if you look at the life of the apostle Paul long enough, you will see what one person can do. He affected people from the simplest man on the street to the leaders of Rome. It is amazing to see the impact of one man's dedicated life.

8. The providence of God

The providence of God is the marvelous way in which God works out all human circumstances to achieve His own results.

9. The Christian's attitude toward government (see pp. 90-91)

10. The Christian's attitude toward persecution (see p. 92)

Lesson

Acts 25:1-12 describes the defense of Paul before Festus. The former governor, Felix, had been assigned by the Roman government to rule over the Jewish people but had been recalled to Rome because of poor leadership. Felix was unfit in his position as governor as were the earlier governors before him. He, like Pontius Pilate before him, had been forced to make some decisions that were favorable to the Jewish leaders. According to historians, Felix was so inept that the whole province of Judea was in an uproar. Riots were occurring repeatedly with villages being burned, looted, and plundered. The Jews wanted to get rid of Felix, and, consequently, Rome recalled him in dishonor in A.D. 59 and replaced him with Porcius Festus. This is indicated in Acts 24:27: "After two years [two years into Paul's imprisonment] Porcius Festus came into Felix's place."

Felix left Paul in prison because he wanted to pacify the Jewish leaders, although Paul had never been accused of anything. Festus inherited not only the political problems of Felix's regime but the prisoner of Felix as well. Historians do not record much about Festus other than that he was a good administrator. Josephus, probably the most informed and widely read historian of that period of history, implied that Festus was better than Felix and Albinus, who followed Festus as governor (*Antiquities* 20.8.9—20.9.2). Unlike Felix, Festus dealt with things as swiftly as possible. He died after only two years in office. The account of his dealings with the apostle Paul are recorded in Acts 25:1-12.

I. THE ASSASSINATION PLOTTED (vv. 1-5)

A. The Unfortunate Legacy (v. 1)

"Now when Festus was come into the province, after three days he ascended from Caesarea to Jerusalem."

Festus has to be pitied somewhat because his predecessor's incompetency left him a legacy of profound hate from the

Jewish people, who hated all their oppressors. The incompetency of the previous governors didn't help matters at all. Festus arrived on the scene in Caesarea, which was the Roman headquarters. The Romans had taken over the palace of Herod the Great and turned it into the Roman praetorium, where the governor lived and ruled. He spent three days there getting things organized and becoming oriented to his surroundings.

1. The ascension

   After a brief three days in Caesarea, Festus recognized the need to "ascend" to Jerusalem. In the land of Palestine you were always "ascending" to Jerusalem because of its elevation. Festus went to Jerusalem because he knew the first thing he had to do in office was to conciliate the Jewish population.

2. The animosity

   The animosity toward Felix and the Roman Empire was so extensive and hostile that Festus went to Jerusalem, the national center of Israel, to acquaint himself with the Sanhedrin. He knew he had to become well aware of the customs and politics in the situation in which he had been thrust. He knew those contacts were important, so he went to Jerusalem to establish a warm, working relationship between himself and the Sanhedrin.

   a) Against Pilate

      The Romans were afraid of the Jews. The previous Roman governors had been severely scorned by the Jewish leaders, who were masters at blackmail. They blackmailed Pilate into crucifying Jesus Christ. The first thing Pilate did when he arrived in Judea was ride into Jerusalem with idols all over his armor, intending to place them all over the area. They were idols in the image of Caesar, which made the Jews extremely upset. He refused to take the idols down, so the Jewish leaders reported him to Rome, who ordered him to take them down.

      From the beginning of his reign, Pilate was under the thumbs of the Jewish leaders. When he threatened to kill them, they called his bluff, and he backed down. When it came time to crucify Jesus Christ, they had Pilate right where they wanted him. If he failed to do what they wanted, they would report him to Rome again, and his reign would be over. They had Pilate cornered from the time he arrived.

b) Against Felix

The Jewish leaders had Felix in the same situation. He was afraid to do what was right concerning the apostle Paul because if he had, they would have been upset and would have reported him to Rome. Felix was not able to handle them.

c) Against Antiochus Epiphanes

The Romans could look back into Jewish history and see the Jews' animosity toward their oppressors. If you study the intertestamental period, the four-hundred-year period between the Old and New Testaments, you'll see that Israel was dominated largely by Syria. Syrian King Antiochus Epiphanes, who liked to call himself *Theos Epiphanes*, which means "God manifest," was enamored with Greek culture and tried to impose it on the Jews. However, the Jews called him *Epimanes*, which means "the maniac." They finally revolted in a movement led by Judas Maccabaeus and his sons and started a revolution that ultimately led to liberation from Syrian rule.

The Romans knew the revolutionary power the Jews had, and if they could ever mount a charge, the Roman Empire would be in a battle. Every Roman governor was walking a tightrope. When Festus arrived, he knew it was strategic to conciliate the Jewish leaders and at the same time not get himself under their thumb. He immediately went to Jerusalem to work on this conciliation.

B. The Unwise Leadership (vv. 2-3)

"Then the high priest and the chief of the Jews informed him against Paul, and besought him, and desired a favor against him, that he would send him to Jerusalem, laying wait in the way to kill him."

1. The request motivated by their hatred

The first order of business for the leaders was to discuss with Festus the situation of the apostle Paul. The term "the chief of the Jews" refers to the Sanhedrin, which consisted of the high priest, chief priests, elders, and scribes. There were seventy-one in all.

Verse 2 says they "informed him against Paul." That's the

first thing they said to the new governor. Over two years had passed in Paul's imprisonment, and the first thing they said to Festus had to do with Paul. That question had been burning in their minds for over two years.

Verse 2 ends by saying they "besought him." Why did they beseech him? They "desired a favor against him" (v. 3). The one thing the Jewish leaders did not want in Paul's case was justice. They wanted a favor because justice would have released him. The leaders requested that Festus "send him to Jerusalem" (v. 3). Initially, that request sounds innocent. But they were planning to lay "wait in the way to kill him" (v. 3). It was a planned ambush. The Jews were trying to take advantage of the new governor. They knew Festus realized the mistakes Felix had made and that he wanted to appease them. They were ready to trap Festus from the beginning of his rule.

The Sanhedrin operated in a deceptive way. If the plot to execute Paul was carried out and they later wanted to rid themselves of Festus, they could report to Rome that he should be replaced because he was responsible for the death of an innocent man. It is amazing to note that Paul had been in prison for two years, and yet they were still terrified about anyone who preached Christ. There is little doubt that word of Paul's present ministry came to Jerusalem from Caesarea. Paul must have taught and ministered quite extensively. The word around Jerusalem must have been that Paul was doing well living in the Caesarean palace. The possibility of a new governor brought with it the possibility of release, but the Jews were afraid of that.

2. The reasons motivating their hatred

    a) The hatred of religious people toward Christianity

        It is amazing that the religious leaders of Paul's time were the great antagonists to Christianity. They claimed to love God and yet had murder on their minds. Religion is mild until it comes in conflict with the truth. The struggle is not between false religions fighting among themselves but between the false systems and the truth. The only desire of the religious leaders was a favor from the governor, not justice. They were hoping that the new governor's inexperience would play a part in the execution of Paul.

(1) The origin of false religion

Whenever you see hatred like that, it is of satanic origin. The reason religious people hate the truth is that they are in Satan's false religious system. His system is against Christ. The Jewish leaders despised Paul because he identified himself with Jesus Christ, not because he was dishonoring the Jewish people. He was once one of them—chosen for their own court, a leader of the Christian persecution, and a student of the great Rabbi Gamaliel. But when he became identified with Jesus Christ they hated him, not for his sake but for Christ's sake. The hatred of so-called religious people is always toward the truth.

(2) The origin of false doctrine

If you read through the New Testament you will find that the greatest persecution comes from false teachers. They slander the truth, as Paul told Timothy (1 Tim. 1:6-7).

(a) John 15:18-25—Jesus said, "If the world hate you, ye know that it hated me before it hated you. If ye were of the world, the world would love its own; but because ye are not of the world, but I have chosen you out of the world, therefore the world hateth you. Remember the word that I said unto you, The servant is not greater than his lord. If they have persecuted me, they will also persecute you; if they have kept my saying, they will keep yours also. But all these things will they do unto you for my name's sake, because they know not him that sent me. If I had not come and spoken unto them, they had not had sin; but now they have no cloak for their sin. He that hateth me hateth my Father also. If I had not done among them the works which no other man did, they had not had sin; but now have they both seen and hated me and my Father. But this cometh to pass, that the word might be fulfilled that is written in their law, They hated me without a cause."

If you were to give a definition of the word *world* (Gk., *kosmos*), what would you say? Most would think immediately of Satan's evil system. But when you think of the world as Satan's evil system, don't just think of bars, crime, prostitution, and immorality; think primarily of religion. That is the pinnacle of Satan's system. The Bible says that Satan disguises himself as an angel of light (2 Cor. 11:14). Most of the hatred toward Jesus Christ does not come from atheism but from religion. Those that hated Christ were not the prostitutes or criminals but the religious leaders.

If you are a part of the world, the people of the world will love you (v. 19). If you are a part of the "big beer brotherhood," everyone is your buddy. All you have to do is drink beer, and you are a part of the brotherhood. You can get drunk like everyone else and be one of the boys. The implication is that if you don't drink beer, you're out of it.

The world has ways of recognizing its own. The world hates us because of Christ (v. 19). The world may hate you because of something other than Christ, but the hatred Christ is talking about in verses 18-25 is the world's animosity toward the truth of Jesus Christ. And the only way that kind of persecution can happen is when you legitimately live a godly life. All religious people claim to know God, but they don't know Him if they don't know Christ (vv. 20-21). That is why people despise Christ and all who follow Him.

(b) John 16:9—The great and climactic sin of John 15:22 is explained in John 16:9, which says the Holy Spirit will convict worldly people of sin "because they believe not." If Jesus had never come and confronted sinners, He would not have unmasked the truth that they were not believers. John 15:24 describes the sin of rejecting the full revelation of Christ. Christ was saying, "I manifested

Myself and made people responsible for their sin. I have shown them to be unbelievers by their rejection of the truth." He says at the end of verse 25 that they hated Him without a cause because of their sin. The world hates people who stand in opposition to Christ.

(3) The origin of false teachers (see p. 78)

b) The power of a blameless life

Your life should be a rebuke to the world. A friend told me he once shared Christ with a man so frequently and showed such concern that the man became angry with him and wouldn't speak to him for years. However, the wife of that man received Jesus Christ just from the testimony of my friend's witness. She saw how angry her husband became, so she had to investigate the claims of Christ. She began to read the Bible and received Christ. Now they're praying for her husband.

Aristeides the Just

Aristeides was a man who lived in Athens during the fifth century B.C. He was called "the Just." The Greek word for *just* means "righteous." He was such a good man that people gave him the name Aristeides the Just. The people of Athens, along with the council of Athens, voted to have him banished from the city. When one of the citizens was asked why he had voted for the banishment, he replied, "Because I am tired of hearing him referred to as 'the Just.'" He could not stand anyone who was upright. It is dangerous to live a godly life in an ungodly system.

A godly life stands as a conscience to the watching world, pricking its conscience. The world will be a terrible place during the Tribulation period because the conscience of the world (Christians) will be taken in the rapture, and all hell will literally break loose. The convicting power of a blameless life can be seen in Acts 25:2. For two years the Jewish leaders hated Paul, and their bitterness was like venom, eating away their hearts. That hatred was to be meted out against the apostle Paul.

c) The power of sin

There is another principle here, and it is that sin enslaves people to its power. For two years the Jews had been bound by sin in thinking how to destroy the apostle Paul. The sad thing about the deceitfulness of sin is that if you are an unbeliever, you think you're free, but you're really enslaved.

The Soaring Eagle

There is an old story of a man watching an eagle soaring beautifully across the sky. As he watched, it flew lower and lower until finally its wings began to fold and flap like a sparrow's. Suddenly it smashed into the side of a cliff. The man walked over and picked it up, and there clutching its breast was a rodent that had sucked out its blood. That is what sin is like. We think we are getting away with our sin, yet little by little the life is being drained out of us. Sin enslaves the human heart.

Paul had been in jail for two years, and instead of the Jewish leaders being free to love, they were slaves to hate. As Dr. S. I. McMillan has said, "It's not what you eat—its what eats you" (*None of These Diseases*, [Old Tappan, N.J.: Revell, 1984], p. 105). One of the greatest evils is hate. You will self-destruct if you continue to feel hatred or bitterness toward someone.

(1) Romans 6:16—Paul said, "Know ye not that to whom ye yield yourselves servants to obey, his servants ye are whom ye obey; whether of sin unto death, or of obedience unto righteousness?" If you say yes to sin, you become the slave of sin.

(2) Genesis 4:5-7—This is what hate did to Cain: "Unto Cain and to his offering he [God] had not respect. And Cain was very angry, and his countenance fell. And the Lord said unto Cain, Why art thou angry? And why is thy countenance fallen? If thou doest well, shalt thou not be accepted? And if thou doest not well, sin lieth at the door. And unto thee shall be his desire, and thou shalt rule over him."

(3) Genesis 27:41—Esau is another example of someone whom hate drove his entire life. The Scripture says, "Esau hated Jacob because of the blessing with which his father blessed him: and Esau said in his heart, The days of mourning for my father are at hand; then will I slay my brother, Jacob."

4) Genesis 37:8—"His [Joseph's] brethren said to him, Shalt thou indeed . . . have dominion over us? And they hated him yet the more for his dreams, and for his words." Hate caused the sons of Jacob to sell their brother Joseph into slavery.

5) 1 Samuel 18:7-9—"The women spoke to one another as they played, and said, Saul hath slain his thousands, and David his ten thousands. And Saul was very angry, and the saying displeased him; and he said, They have ascribed unto David ten thousands, and to me they have ascribed but thousands; and what he have more, but the kingdom? And Saul watched enviously David, from that day and onward." Hatred for David ultimately drove Saul to kill himself.

6) 2 Samuel 13:22, 28—Hate led Absalom to kill his brother Amnon. Scripture says, "Absalom spoke unto his brother, Amnon, neither good nor bad; for Absalom hated Amnon, because he had forced his sister, Tamar. . . . Absalom had commanded his servants, saying, Mark ye, now, when Amnon's heart is merry with wine, and when I say unto you, Smite Amnon; then kill him, fear not. Have not I commanded you? Be courageous, and be valiant."

Sin is the cruel master of slavery. What starts out as a simple activity becomes a habit that produces slavery. That is the deceitfulness of sin. The only One who can break the power of sin is Jesus Christ. There is no human resource that can handle this kind of enslavement. When you give your life to Jesus Christ, sin's power is broken. Those who have known only hatred before are now able to love.

C. The Unforeseen Limitation (vv. 4-5)

"But Festus answered, that Paul should be kept at Caesarea, and that he himself would depart shortly for there. Let them, therefore, said he, who among you are able, go down with me, and accuse this man, if there be any wickedness in him."

1. The proposal

It might seem initially a fair request to ask Festus to take Paul to Jerusalem for a trial. But Festus was an intelligent man and might have suspected some wrong motives on the part of the Jewish leaders. He informed them that he intended to leave Paul in Caesarea and try his case there. If any accusation was to be made, it was to be made in Caesarea. Festus probably had an instinct for justice by the very fact of his position. Also, history implies he had a commendable character.

When you begin to look at the evidence surrounding the trial, it is strange that Festus didn't take Paul to Jerusalem. It seemed a rather insignificant request. Festus was probably aware of Jewish procedure and wanted to make friends with the Jewish leaders. He didn't know Paul personally, so his reputation as a subversive hadn't had its full impact on Festus. All these factors contributed to Paul's staying at Caesarea.

2. The plan

There was another reason for Festus's not taking Paul to Jerusalem: the providence of God.

a) The providence of God

God ordains the attitudes and actions of men to bring about His own end. Even in government, God is in sovereign control. Some may wonder why God does what He does in certain situations, but you can still trust Him. If you do not understand what God is doing, attribute it to your ignorance and not His ineptitude. People are so anxious about the direction of the world, but God is in control. I never worry about politics, the economy, or the world because I trust in the God who is in control of the world. There are many passages in Scripture that show God is in control of the world.

(1) John 19:10-11—Pilate said to Jesus, "Speakest thou not unto me? Knowest thou not that I have power to crucify thee, and have power to release thee? Jesus answered, Thou couldest have no power at all against me, except it were given thee from above." Pilate thought he was running the show, but he wasn't—God was.

(2) Acts 2:22-23—The apostle Peter said, "Ye men of Israel, hear these words: Jesus of Nazareth, a man approved of God among you by miracles and wonders and signs, which God did by him in

the midst of you, as ye yourselves also know; him, being delivered by the determinate counsel and foreknowledge of God." God is in complete control.

(3) John 7:30—The religious leaders sought to take Jesus, "but no man laid hands on him, because his hour was not yet come." God was timing things perfectly.

(4) Luke 22:53—Jesus said, "When I was daily with you in the temple, ye stretched forth no hands against me; but this is your hour, and the power of darkness." The Jewish leaders had tried to catch Jesus but couldn't. He passed through their midst, and then in effect said, "Now you may take Me." God ordained the entire event.

(5) Genesis 45:7-8—Joseph said to his brothers, "God sent me before you to preserve you a posterity in the earth, and to save your lives by a great deliverance. So now it was not you that sent me here, but God: and he hath made me a father to Pharaoh, and lord of all his house, and a ruler throughout all the land of Egypt." The brothers of Joseph sold him into slavery in Egypt, where he later became a ruler. Who really put Joseph in Egypt? It was not his brothers but God. Do you know what would have happened if Joseph had never gotten to Egypt? All his brothers might have died in the famine that came, and the messianic line would have been obliterated. God preserved the messianic line by sending Joseph in advance to Egypt to make sure that when the famine came, Joseph would have Egypt stocked with enough extra wheat to feed his family. That is God's providence. God uses natural circumstances to effect His supernatural desires.

(6) Daniel 4:17—King Nebuchadnezzar said of Babylon, "This matter is by the decree of the watchers, and the demand by the word of the holy ones, to the intent that the living may know that the Most High ruleth in the kingdom of men, and giveth it to whomsoever he will, and setteth up over it the basest of men." Nebuchadnezzar had the idea that he was the greatest ruler, but he had a vision

that Babylon would fall to the Medes and the Persians, who would be followed by the Greeks, and finally by the Romans. These were the four great world empires. But to whomever is in charge, verse 17 says, "That the living may know that the Most High [God] ruleth in the kingdom of men, and giveth it to whomsoever he will." Do you know who is running the politics of the United States of America behind the scenes, to effect His own will, even through the evil of men? God. The powers that be are ordained of God (Rom. 13:1). We may not always understand what God is doing, but we can trust Him.

Daniel 4:25 says, "Till thou know that the Most High ruleth in the kingdom of men, and giveth it to whomsoever he will." Verse 32 says the same thing: "Until thou know that the Most High ruleth in the kingdom of men, and giveth it to whomsoever he will." If God said something once, it's important; but if God said something three times, you had better remember it. Verse 35 says, "All the inhabitants of the earth are reputed as nothing, and he doeth according to his will in the army of heaven, and among the inhabitants of the earth."

Daniel 5:21 says, "Till he knew that the Most High God ruled in the kingdom of men, and that he appointed over it whomsoever he will." God rules the kingdoms of men. That is the greatest political fact in existence. God is ruling and in control of destiny. Festus didn't do what he wanted because God was in control, and if Paul had gone to Jerusalem, there would have been an ambush, and Paul would have been killed. God made a promise to Paul that he would bear witness to Christ in Rome (Acts 23:11).

b) The place of defense

Verse 5 says, "Let them, therefore, said he, who among you are able, go down with me, and accuse this man, if there be any wickedness in him." The phrase "who among you are able" is *dunatai* in the Greek text and refers to those men who are powerful or influential in their position. Festus was asking the powerful Jewish men of the Sanhedrin to come down to Caesarea and accuse Paul there and see if there was any wickedness in him.

I. THE ACCUSATION PRESENTED (vv. 6-7)

"When he had tarried among them more than ten days, he went down unto Caesarea; and the next day, sitting on the judgment seat, commanded Paul to be brought. And when he was come, the Jews who came down from Jerusalem stood round about, and laid many and grievous complaints against Paul."

A. The Accusations

1. Sedition (see pp. 25-28)

   Acts 24:5-6 describes the accusations brought against Paul two years earlier. The first accusation was that Paul was a "pestilent fellow, and a mover of sedition among all the Jews throughout the world." They claimed he was stirring up Jewish revolution against Rome, which is the crime of insurrection.

2. Sectarianism (see pp. 28-34)

   The second accusation brought against Paul in Acts 24:5 is that he was "a ringleader of the sect of the Nazarenes." That means they thought Paul was not only a political activist but a heretic as well.

3. Sacrilege (see pp. 41-44)

   In Acts 24:6 Paul is accused of going "about to profane the temple." Paul was not only accused of being a political activist and a heretic but also of being sacrilegious by abandoning Judaism.

B. The Application (see p. 81)

According to the Jewish leaders, Paul had offended Rome, Israel, and God. But all three accusations were lies. I trust this lesson shows you the power of a totally dedicated life—the life of the apostle Paul—and that God will use the principles that we've studied to cause you to glorify Him.

Focusing on the Facts

1. How many defenses did Paul make? Describe the phases of his trials beginning at Jerusalem (see pp. 56-57).
2. With what does Acts 21-28 deal (see p. 57)?
3. Name the principles taught in Acts 25:1-12 (see pp. 57-59).

4. What is the power of a blameless life (see p. 57)?
5. Describe the principle of the hatred of religious people toward Christianity (see pp. 57-58).
6. What does it mean to be a slave to sin (see p. 58)?
7. One of the lost virtues for many Christians is_____(see p. 58).
8. Describe the principle of the exoneration of Christianity (see p. 58).
9. What can be the impact of one man's totally committed life (see p. 58)?
10. What is meant by the providence of God (see p. 59)?
11. What was the condition of the government Festus inherited from Felix (see p. 59)?
12. What was the first order of business for Festus (see p. 60)?
13. What was the first order of business for the Sanhedrin (see p. 61)?
14. What was the underlying motive of the Sanhedrin in wanting Paul's trial in Jerusalem (see p. 62)?
15. Who is the origin of all false systems of religion (see pp. 62-63)?
16. A godly life stands as a_____to the watching world (see p. 65).
17. What is one of the greatest evils, according to page 66?
18. What was the unforeseen limitation not expected by the Jewish leaders (see p. 68)?
19. Who is in control of all governments of the world? Support your answer with Scripture (see pp. 68-69).
20. What were the three things Paul was accused of in his trial (see p. 71)?

Pondering the Principles

1. Several principles were brought out in the text of Acts 25:1-7, one of which was the hatred of religious people toward Christianity. Can you see any evidence of hatred by others toward you because you are a Christian? If not, what is hindering you from being salt and light in your workplace or community (Matt. 5:13-16)? Read John 15:18-24 and ask God to allow you the joyous opportunity of suffering for Christ's sake. Take each verse of this passage once a day for seven days, and thank God for the opportunity to suffer for Christ.

2. Another principle we studied was the power of a blameless life. Do you have a blameless Christian testimony with those around you? Is it evident to everyone you come in contact with that you are a Christian and that you live a life that rebukes the world of

its sin? If that is not the pattern of your life, ask God to make you the kind of person that lives a consistent Christian testimony. Memorize Colossians 3:1-4 and strive to make it the pattern of your life.

3. There are several reasons Festus did not take Paul to Jerusalem to be tried, but the overarching reason is the principle of God's providence. God ordains the attitudes and actions of men to bring about His own end, yet man is still responsible for the choices he makes. Do you trust the sovereign God for what He is doing in your life? Are you being responsible in making godly decisions? Reread the account of Joseph in Genesis 37, and ask God to make your responses to His will like the responses of Joseph (Gen. 45:7-8).

5

Paul Before Festus—Part 2
The Power of a Dedicated Life

Outline

Review
I. The Assassination Plotted (vv.1-5)
   A. The Unfortunate Legacy (v. 1)
   B. The Unwise Leadership (vv. 2-3)
      1. The real request motivated by their hatred
      2. The real reason motivating their hatred
         a) The hatred of religious people toward Christianity
            (1) The origin of false religion
            (2) The origin of false doctrine
            (3) The origin of false teachers
         b) The power of a blameless life
         c) The power of sin
            (1) John 8:30-32
            (2) Titus 3:3
            (3) Romans 6:19
   C. The Unforeseen Limitation (vv. 4-5)
      1. The proposal
      2. The plan
         a) The providence of God
         b) The place of defense
II. The Accusation Presented (vv. 6-7)
   A. The Accusations
      1. Sedition
      2. Sectarianism
      3. Sacrilege
   B. The Application
      1. False persecution
      2. Faulty persecution

Lesson

III. The Absence of Proof (vv. 7-11)
  A. The Lack of Evidence
  B. The Lesson of Paul
    1. The power of a blameless life
      a) Be right
      b) Speak right
      c) Think right
    2. The exoneration of Christianity
      a) The zealots of the Jewish religion
      b) The zenith of the Roman Empire
      c) The lunacy of Nero
      d) The loyalty of Christians
        (1) Acts 16:35-39
        (2) Acts 18:12-16
        (3) 1 Peter 2:12-14
  C. The Logic of Paul
  D. The Limitation of Festus
  E. The Language of Paul
IV. The Appeal Proposed (v. 12)
  A. The Proposal
    1. Paul's right
    2. Paul's reasoning
    3. Paul's risk
  B. The Principles
    1. The courage of the committed Christian
      a) Numbers 13:30-33
      b) Judges 4:8-9
      c) 1 Samuel 17:32
    2. The Christian's attitude toward government
    3. The Christian's attitude toward persecution
    4. The impact of the totally committed life

Review

Acts 25:1-12 describes the apostle Paul's trial before Festus. The book of Acts contains many principles that are not obvious but under the surface of the text. In a book of the Bible that contains historical narrative, most of the doctrine is implied or illustrated. An example is this portion of the book of Acts, where there is no particular statement regarding any doctrine, and yet there are several principles that can be seen in this passage.

In the last chapter we saw eight principles that come from the passage without specifically being stated, yet they are implied.

A. The Power of a Blameless Life (see p. 57)

B. The Hatred of Religious People Toward Christianity (see pp. 57-58)

C. The Power of Sin (see p. 58)

D. The Pattern of Persecution from the World (see p. 58)

E. The Courage of a Committed Christian (see p. 58)

F. The Exoneration of Christianity (see p. 58)

G. The Impact of the Totally Committed Life (see p. 58)

H. The Providence of God (see p. 59)

None of these principles are new in Scripture. They are all stated in various portions of the book of Acts, and it is as if the Holy Spirit puts this narrative in Acts 25 as a reminder. Second Peter 1:12 says, "I will not be negligent to put you always in remembrance of these things, though ye know them, and are established in the present truth." The Holy Spirit wants to remind the reader of the book of Acts about these principles. They are summed up in Acts 25:1-12.

I. THE ASSASSINATION PLOTTED (vv. 1-5; see pp. 59-71)

"Now when Festus was come into the province, after three days he ascended from Caesarea to Jerusalem. Then the high priest and the chief of the Jews informed him against Paul, and besought him, and desired a favor against him, that he would send him to Jerusalem, laying wait in the way to kill him. But Festus answered, that Paul should be kept at Caesarea, and that he himself would depart shortly for there. Let them, therefore, said he, who among you are able, go down with me, and accuse this man, if there by any wickedness in him."

A. The Unfortunate Legacy (v. 1; see pp. 59-61)

The apostle Paul had been accused by the Jewish leaders of three things: sedition—committing crimes against Rome; sectarianism—being a heretic; and sacrilege—blaspheming God by desecrating the Temple. Those accusations were all without evidence, yet were made nonetheless. As a result, Paul found himself before the governor, Felix, to be tried. Felix knew Paul was innocent, but he did not want to upset the Jewish leaders, who wanted him dead. As a result, Felix kept him in prison for two years. At the end of that time, Felix was removed from his assignment in disgrace and taken back to Rome, and a new man, Festus, was put in his place.

As Acts 25 opens, Festus arrives in Caesarea to take over his responsibility. Caesarea was the location of the head of the Roman government in Judea. He performed some business there for three days and then headed for Jerusalem. Festus knew it was important for him to establish relationships with the Jewish people. He also knew that relationships had been very shaky with Felix, and it was important to form a smooth working relationship in the beginning of his rule. The first item the Jewish leaders brought up when Festus arrived was the apostle Paul. He had already been a prisoner for two years, and because of their deep hatred for him they wanted Paul dead. They spoke to a naive and uninformed Festus and asked him to bring Paul to Jerusalem. They really wanted to ambush Paul on the way. But Festus refused, saying, "Let them, therefore . . . who among you are able, go down with me, and accuse this man, if there be any wickedness in him" (v. 5).

B. The Unwise Leadership (vv. 2-3; see p. 61)

1. The request motivated by their hatred (see pp. 61-62)

2. The reason motivating their hatred (see pp. 62-67)

   a) The hatred of religious people toward Christianity (see pp. 62-65)

   The first principle in Acts 25:1-12 is the hatred of religious people toward Christianity. The people who were antagonistic toward Paul were not Christians; they were just outwardly religious.

   (1) The origin of false religion (see p. 63)

   The persecution that comes against true religion most often comes from those in false religions. It is when false religion rears its ugly head that it begins to abuse the truth. Satan disguises himself as an angel of light (2 Cor. 11:14) and propagates all systems of false religion in antagonism toward true Christianity. The most obvious enemy of Christ is false religion. Throughout the book of Acts, it is the Jewish religious leaders who persecute Christ's followers.

   Persecution always comes as the result of a religious issue. Religion is always the persecutor of Christianity. Satan opposes true religion by setting up false religions and bringing unbelievers into his system in opposition to the truth. That is why any notion of an ecumenical movement is ridiculous because then you have false religions trying to unite with the truth. Jesus said, "He that is not with me is against me; and he that gathereth not with me scattereth abroad" (Matt. 12:30). Christianity is a rebuke to all other religions in the world, and as Christians, we cannot accommodate them. There can be no fellowship with those in opposition to Christianity.

(2) The origin of false doctrine (see pp. 63-65)

(3) The origin of false teachers

Second Peter 2:1-2 says, "There were false prophets also among the people, even as there shall be false teachers among you, who secretly shall bring in destructive heresies, even denying the Lord that bought them, and bring upon themselves swift destruction. And many shall follow their pernicious ways, by reason of whom the way of truth shall be evil spoken of."

Throughout the history of Israel, you will find that the biggest problem the Jewish people ever had was their involvement with pagan religions. They were always drifting into all sorts of idolatry, including Baal worship. It was no different in Peter's day (2 Pet. 2:1-2). False teachers will always speak evil of the truth. The only way Christianity will ever get along with false religion is for false religions to abandon their evil and follow the truth. Christianity always stands isolated because all systems of religion in the world are against Christ. Someone might say, "Well, they don't seem to be." That is the point. They secretly bring in destructive heresies that are not always obvious. Some religions are violently anti-Christ; others are more subtle. Think of the church that follows Jesus as a moral teacher but not as God in human flesh. There is no way Christians can ever accommodate people in false religious systems. They must be confronted.

b) The power of a blameless life (see p. 65)

c) The power of sin (see pp. 65-67)

The religious leaders in Israel didn't have to deal with the apostle Paul for two years because of his imprisonment, yet their hatred for him grew. You would think in two years they would have forgotten about him, but when Festus arrived, the first thing they said to him concerned Paul (v. 2). They wanted him dead. They asked Festus to send him to Jerusalem so they could ambush him on the way. That kind of attitude says a lot about hatred. Sin drives itself deep into the human heart and stays there only to be released by the Lord Jesus Christ.

(1) John 8:30-32—Scripture says, "As he spoke these words, many believed on him. Then said Jesus to those Jews who believed on him, If ye continue in my word, then are ye my disciples indeed; and ye shall know the truth, and the truth shall make you free." Jesus in effect was saying, "I'm glad you believe in Me but the proof of true faith is if you continue in My Word. If you're truly saved, the truth will make you free." By saying that, Jesus implied that the Jews were not free but slaves to sin. The Jewish leaders didn't like that and said, "We are Abraham's seed, and were never in bondage to any man. How sayest thou, Ye shall be made free?" (v. 33). They thought that because they were of Jewish heritage, they were absolutely free. They had forgotten about the Egyptians, Babylonians, Medo-Persians, Syrians, Grecians, and Romans. They had been in bondage to many nations. "Jesus answered them, Verily, verily, I say unto you, Whosoever committeth sin is the servant of sin" (v. 34). Sin is slavery that binds the soul. The Greek word for "servant" is *doulos,* meaning "bondslave." The only way you could cease being a bondslave was to die (Kenneth S. Wuest, *Wuest's Word Studies from the Greek New Testament,* vol. 3 [Grand Rapids: Eerdmans, 1973], p. 45). Our Lord said sin is bondage.

(2) Titus 3:3—Paul said, "We ourselves also were once foolish, disobedient, deceived, serving various lusts and pleasures, living in malice and

envy, hateful, and hating one another." Sinners
are called *douloi*, or bondslaves, to lust.

(3) Romans 6:19—Paul also said, "I speak after the
manner of men because of the infirmity of your
flesh; for as ye have yielded your members servants to uncleanness and to iniquity." Sin cap-
tures a man. He is not free but a slave. The only
release from the slavery is death. It is wonderful
to realize that as a believer, you have been
crucified with Jesus Christ, freed from death, and
risen with Him in the likeness of His resurrection
(Rom. 6:3-7). You have become a *doulos* to a new
Master. You do not serve sin but Jesus Himself.
You are still a bondslave, but now you are a
bondslave to Jesus Christ. Being a bondslave to
Christ is better than being a slave to sin. It is sad
that the Jewish leaders would allow two years to
elapse and be destroyed on the inside by their
hatred. Paul, on the other hand, loved them.

C. The Unforeseen Limitation (vv. 4-5; see pp. 68-71)

1. The proposal (see p. 68)

2. The plan (see pp. 68-71)

a) The providence of God (see pp. 68-70)

In spite of what seemed to be the normal course of
events, God was ordering the entire sequence of
Paul's trials. When the Jewish leaders wanted Festus
to take Paul up to Jerusalem, he refused. That was
very strange because Festus was trying to win the
Jews over. He was trying to influence them and
establish a base of operation. But instead of saying
yes to their request, Festus said no. There wasn't any
logical reason to say no, other than the fact that God
was in control. Lamentations 3:37-38 says, "Who is
he who saith, and it cometh to pass, when the Lord
commandeth it not? Out of the mouth of the Most
High proceedeth not evil and good?" It is clear in the
Word of God that nothing happens for good or evil
unless it is in the framework of God's allowance.
Festus didn't realize it, but he was moving right along
the divine timetable, and his actions fit into God's
plan. God controls the destiny of every man.

b) The place of defense (see p. 71)

II. THE ACCUSATION PRESENTED (vv. 6-7; see p.71)

"And when he had tarried among them more than ten days, he went down unto Caesarea; and the next day, sitting on the judgment seat, commanded Paul to be brought. And when he was come, the Jews who came down from Jerusalem stood round about, and laid many and grievous complaints against Paul, which they could not prove."

A. The Accusations (see p. 71)

1. Sedition

2. Sectarianism

3. Sacrilege

B. The Application

The best original manuscripts render verse 6 as saying, "When he had tarried among them more than eight or ten days." So in the space of eight or ten days, Festus had made some contacts with the Jewish leaders and established relationships with the high priest and the Sanhedrin. When he went back down to Caesarea, he dealt with Paul the very next day. The accusers came from Jerusalem ready to present their case, but all their complaints were without evidence. The kind of accusations that the Jewish leaders presented against Paul are typical of the persecution that comes from the world.

1. False persecution

In Matthew 5:11 Jesus says, "Blessed are ye, when men shall revile you, and persecute you, and shall say all manner of evil against you falsely, for my sake." Jesus was saying, "It isn't you they hate, it's Me."

2. Faulty persecution

If a Christian receives the rebuke of the world as Paul received it, it will not be because he deserves it but because of his vibrant testimony for Christ. His life should be lived in such a way that any accusation brought against him is false. The world brings accusations because they cannot tolerate Christ in us. If our lives are blameless, the world will take notice.

Lesson

III. THE ABSENCE OF PROOF (vv. 7-11)

"And when he was come, the Jews who came down from

84

Jerusalem stood round about, and laid many and grievous complaints against Paul, which they could not prove. While he answered for himself, Neither against the law of the Jews, neither against the temple, nor yet against Caesar, have I offended in anything at all. But Festus, willing to do the Jews a favor, answered Paul, and said, Wilt thou go up to Jerusalem, and there be judged of these things before me? Then said Paul, I stand at Caesar's judgment seat, where I ought to be judged; to the Jews have I done no wrong, as thou very well knowest. For if I be an offender, or have committed anything worthy of death, I refuse not to die; but if there be none of these things of which these accuse me, no man may deliver me unto them. I appeal unto Caesar."

A. The Lack of Evidence

According to Scripture, the accusations against Paul could not be proved (v. 7). In all the trials of Paul thus far, there was never any substantiated evidence, only trumped up false charges. They could not prove one charge against Paul. There were no witnesses, no evidence, and therefore no case. Some have suggested that the Jewish leaders did not really work hard enough at convicting Paul, but that theory is not supported in Scripture. In chapters 23 and 24, the Jewish leaders try to gather a case against Paul with no evidence. They are attempting the same thing in Chapter 25.

Verse 6 says that Festus spent eight or ten days in Jerusalem before returning to Caesarea. A possible reason for the delay in Festus coming back to Caesarea might have been to allow the Jewish leaders to build up their case against Paul. Since the Jewish leaders had lost in two previous trials because of a lack of evidence and witnesses, they must have used most of those eight to ten days scurrying about to produce some evidence. But they couldn't find any because Paul had done nothing wrong.

B. The Lesson of Paul

1. The power of a blameless life

The effect of an innocent and blameless testimony is a powerful rebuke to the world. First Peter 3:14-16 says, "If ye suffer for righteousness' sake, happy are ye; and be not afraid of their terror, neither be troubled, but sanctify the Lord God in your hearts, and be ready always to give an answer to every man that asketh you a reason of the hope that is in you, with meekness and fear, having a good conscience, that, whereas they speak evil of you, as of evildoers, they may be ashamed that falsely accuse your good manner of life in Christ." If you suffer for sin, you deserve the accusation of the world; but if you suffer for the sake of righteousness, you should be happy because you are suffering for Christ.

a) Be right

A Christian is to do three things according to this passage. The first thing, according to verse 14, is that he live a holy life so that the world cannot rightly accuse him of sin.

b) Speak right

Verse 15 commands that a Christian is to speak accurately the truth of God. He is to set apart Christ in his heart and be ready to give an answer to anyone about that truth.

c) Think right

The third command is in verse 16: Have "a good conscience." After you have been persecuted for righteousness' sake and spoken the truth of God, your conscience ought to be clear because you know you have pleased God. The result is that the world will speak evil against you, but they will be ashamed because they are falsely accusing your good manner of life in Christ. Do you know how to rebuke people who accuse you? Give them nothing to accuse you of, and their accusations will be unfounded. Then they will have to face the real issue, which is their hatred of Christianity, not anything you've done wrong.

Paul's innocent life made the Jewish leaders face time and time again the fact that their hearts were not right. Paul forced them to feel that way because there was no crime they could blame him for. According to 1 Peter 3:14-16 you are to examine what you are, say, and think. You are to then set Christ apart, be bold, and confront the world with your innocent life. The impact of such a life can make people ashamed—ashamed enough to cause conviction that may bring them to Christ.

2. The exoneration of Christianity

It was a common tactic of the Jewish leaders to try to destroy Christianity by accusing the Christians of being criminals against the Roman government. Throughout the book of Acts and the early history of the church, the Jewish leaders tried over and over again to make the Romans believe that Christianity was a revolution. They claimed that if Christianity continued, it would overthrow the government. The hypocrisy of it all was that many of those same Jewish leaders were busy trying to overthrow the government.

a) The zealots of the Jewish religion

There was a group called the Zealots who were starting riots and secretly assassinating those they wanted to get rid of. The Zealots would kill any Jew who paid homage to Rome as soon as they would kill a Roman. There was tremendous insurrection coming out of Judaism, and yet the religious leaders were trying to accuse the Christians of insurrection. Every time the Jewish leaders would present a case for the trial of a Christian, the Roman government would declare them innocent.

The testimony of the exoneration of Christianity is written down for all time and for all men to know. Christianity is not a revolution or a political threat but a personal relationship with the living God. The world doesn't need to fear Christianity because God has established that fact in His Word.

b) The zenith of the Roman Empire

The Romans started persecuting Christians because there was a change in the structure of the existing Roman Empire. The Roman Empire was vast, extending from the Euphrates River in Asia on the east to Britain on the west. To the north was Europe and to the south, North Africa. The Romans feared the possible fragmentation of such a large empire, so they needed a unifying factor that would pull the entire empire together. Their solution was Caesar worship. They thought that if they could get everyone to worship Caesar, it might unify the empire. They established the reigning emperor as a god and commanded everyone to worship him. Once a year every inhabitant of the Roman Empire had to take a pinch of incense, burn it to Caesar, and publicly declare Caesar as lord. After that he could worship any god he desired. But no true Christian would worship Caesar, and that presented a difficult problem. So the era of Roman persecution and Christian martyrdom began. The Christians were persecuted for religious disloyalty. False religions always lead the persecution against truth.

c) The lunacy of Nero

The first man to martyr Christians was Nero, who was Caesar at the time of Paul's imprisonment in Caesarea. The first five years of Nero's rule were largely uneventful. Then emperor worship was established, and he brought about large-scale persecution. Nero was a maniac. He began to murder Christians, as did many of the succeeding Caesars, because of supposed religious disloyalty.

d) The loyalty of Christians

The record stands in the Word of God that no guilty verdict was ever found against the believers of that day.

(1) Acts 16:35-39—The Scripture says, "When it was day, the magistrates sent the sergeants, saying, Let those men go. And the keeper of the prison told this saying to Paul, The magistrates have sent to let you go; now, therefore, depart, and go in peace. But Paul said unto them, They have beaten us openly uncondemned, being Romans, and have cast us into prison; and now do they thrust us out privately? Nay verily; but let them come themselves and fetch us out. And the sergeants told these words unto the magistrates; and they feared, when they heard that they were Romans. And they came and besought them, and brought them out, and desired them to depart out of the city." Paul and Silas were thrown in jail for no reason. God caused an earthquake and opened every door in the place (v. 26). The magistrates were frightened because they had been put there without cause. Paul and Silas were upset about being there, yet they accepted it as the will of God. The magistrates wanted Paul and Silas to leave peacefully, but Paul wanted everyone to know that they were placed there illegally. The Roman officials knew Paul and Silas

hadn't done anything, so they wanted to get their own injustice off their back.

    (2) Acts 18:12-16—The Scripture also says, "When Gallio was the deputy of Achaia, the Jews made an attack with one accord against Paul, and brought him to the judgment seat, saying, This fellow persuadeth men to worship God contrary to the law. And when Paul was now about to open his mouth, Gallio said unto the Jews, If it were a matter of wrong or wicked crime, O ye Jews, reason would that I should bear with you. But if it be a question of words and names, and of your law, look ye to it; for I will be no judge of such matters. And he drove them from the judgment seat." Gallio threw the entire case out of court because he realized the case wasn't under his jurisdiction. It is the same throughout the book of Acts. Christians were never convicted by the Roman government of insurrection because a Christian is a model citizen, one who conforms himself to the government for his own conscience's sake.

    (3) 1 Peter 2:12-14—Peter said, "Having your behavior honest among the Gentiles, that, whereas they speak against you as evildoers, they may by your good works, which they shall behold, glorify God in the day of visitation. Submit yourselves to every ordinance of man for the Lord's sake, whether it be to the king, as supreme, or unto governors, as unto them that are sent by him for the punishment of evildoers, and for the praise of them that do well." This is the Christian's responsibility because it gives evidence of a godly testimony. The Christian is to be an example.

C. The Logic of Paul

In Acts 25:8 Paul answers the accusations against himself and effectively ends the case. He said, "Neither against the law of the Jews, neither against the temple, nor yet against Caesar, have I offended in anything at all." The Jewish leaders brought a case into court without any evidence; subsequently, there was no case against Paul.

D. The Limitation of Festus

What should have been Festus's response? He should have
dismissed the case immediately, but instead, "willing to do
the Jews a favor, answered Paul, and said, Wilt thou go up to
Jerusalem, and there be judged of these things before me?"
(v. 9). Festus did what was advantageous for himself by
conciliating the Jewish leaders. If Felix was the procrastinator,
Festus was the governor who did what was expedient, which
is possibly even worse. Festus knew that if he let Paul go, he
would suffer the consequences. The Jewish leaders from the
start of his reign would be against him because they wanted
Paul dead. Festus wanted a compromise: He would allow
Paul to go to Jerusalem only if he himself was the judge. The
Jewish leaders wanted Paul in Jerusalem with the Sanhedrin
judging him.

E. The Language of Paul

Paul was upset by this time and used strong language to
defend himself. He spoke to the governor of the entire Judean
province and said, "I stand at Caesar's judgment seat, where
I ought to be judged; to the Jews have I done no wrong, as
thou very well knowest. For if I be an offender, or have
committed anything worthy of death, I refuse not to die; but
if there be none of these things of which these accuse me, no
man may deliver me unto them" (vv. 10-11).

Any province with a governor sitting on the seat of judgment
was Caesar's representative. Paul is saying in effect, "If
you've got a crime to deal with, then deal with it. I've never
done anything wrong to the Jews, and you know it." Festus
knew Paul had not committed any crime because later in
talking to Agrippa he said, "Against whom, when the
accusers stood up, they brought no accusation of such things
as I supposed" (v. 18). Festus did not let Paul go because of
his political maneuvering.

Paul was a human ping-pong ball between the Roman
governor and the Jewish leaders. They were playing a little
game, and he was the victim. He was no doubt upset at
seeing the absolute naiveté of Festus, who thought the Jewish
leaders would deal nicely with him in Jerusalem. He also
knew that the Jewish leaders would possibly plot to kill him.
He stood trapped in a snake pit of intrigue, victimized by the
two groups and their interplay. He therefore stood up for his
rights as a Roman citizen and asked to be brought before the
highest Roman court.

Paul had tremendous courage. He believed in a principle and stood up for it without compromising. There's quite a difference between Paul and the compromising Jewish leaders. Paul was not trying to escape death. If the charges were true, he was willing to die (v. 11). He knew dying would be a promotion for him (Phil. 1:21). It wasn't death he was avoiding; it was justice that he was after. He knew that under Roman law someone who had not committed a crime was to be set free.

IV. THE APPEAL PROPOSED (v. 12)

"Then Festus, when he had conferred with the council, answered, Hast thou appealed unto Caesar? Unto Caesar shalt thou go."

A. The Proposal

1. Paul's right

The apostle Paul was not making a subtle comment but an official appeal to Caesar. A lower court judgment could be appealed to Caesar either before or after the verdict of a lower court. All the apostle Paul had to do was say, "Ad Caesarum pro voco," or "Caesarum apello," which in Latin means, "I appeal to Caesar," and the case would end. He would immediately be transferred to Rome. That was one of the rights of a Roman citizen, and Paul exercised it. He knew he was getting nowhere in Caesarea in the midst of a political battle. The moment he made his appeal, the case shifted out of the hands of Festus into the hands of Caesar in Rome.

2. Paul's reasoning

Paul must have been excited when his appeal was granted because he knew that it was in the sovereign purpose of God. In Acts 23:11 the Lord says, "Be of good cheer, Paul; for as thou hast testified of me in Jerusalem, so must thou bear witness also at Rome." Paul knew God was controlling his every step, and when he was able to appeal to Caesar, he must have been exhilarated, realizing that this was his ticket to Rome.

3. Paul's risk

Paul's appeal to Caesar was a risk, because the Caesar at that time was Nero himself. If Paul had thought about it long enough, he might have considered himself better off with the expediency of Festus rather than the lunacy of

Nero. Being judged by Nero wasn't the epitome of absolute justice. Nero was one of the most immoral men of that day. He killed Britannicus, the son and heir of the Emperor Claudius. He murdered his mother, Agrippina, to please his lover Poppaea, who was already married. He got angry with Poppaea and killed her by kicking her in the stomach while she was pregnant. He wanted to marry his adopted sister Claudia Antonia, and when she refused, he killed her. He married Statilia Messalina after he assassinated her husband. He spent his career assassinating all the best citizens of Rome because he couldn't stand good people. He finally killed himself, relieving everyone of his despotic rule.

B. The Principles

1. The courage of the committed Christian

The apostle Paul did two courageous deeds: (1) he rebuked Festus face-to-face, and (2) he put himself in the hands of a maniac, Nero. Courage is born out of the confidence a Christian has in God. Paul realized that God could overrule both Festus and Nero. Paul believed that God was running his life, so nothing bothered him.

a) Numbers 13:30-33—The Scripture says, "Caleb stilled the people before Moses, and said, Let us go up at once, and possess it; for we are well able to overcome it" (v. 30). But the other spies said, "There we saw the giants, the sons of Anak, who come of the giants; and we were in our own sight as grasshoppers, and so we were in their sight" (v. 33). Ten out of the twelve spies came back with a grasshopper complex! But Joshua and Caleb came back confident that they could prevail in battle. The difference was courage.

b) Judges 4:8-9—Barak said to Deborah, "If thou wilt go with me, then I will go; but if thou wilt not go with me, then I will not go. And she said, I will surely go with thee: notwithstanding, the journey that thou takest shall not be for thine honor; for the Lord shall sell Sisera into the hand of a woman." The Israelites were vacillating over who was going to defeat Sisera's army. A lady named Deborah took the initiative and led them to victory. All the men blinked and followed. Deborah had courage that God was in control.

c) 1 Samuel 17:32—"David said to Saul, Let no man's heart fail because of him; thy servant will go and fight with this Philistine." David walked up with a handful of rocks to fight a giant. It wasn't that he believed he was a good shot; he believed God would deliver him.

Courage is born out of faith in God, and Paul had that faith. In Acts 20:23-24 Paul says, "The Holy Spirit witnesseth in every city, saying that bonds and afflictions await me. But none of these things move me, neither count I my life dear unto myself, so that I might finish my course with joy, and the ministry, which I have received of the Lord Jesus, to testify the gospel of the grace of God." Courage is irreplaceable for the Christian who is willing to stand up and speak what is true. God will honor that kind of courage. It is a virtue that rightfully belongs to the committed Christian.

2. The Christian's attitude toward government

    Acts 25:12 says, "Festus, when he had conferred with the council, answered, Hast thou appealed unto Caesar? Unto Caesar shalt thou go." Festus had to check with his Roman council to see if Paul had Roman citizenship allowing a legitimate appeal. Festus made the decision for Paul to go to Caesarea, and Paul must have been excited. Rome at last! By this time he had written the book of Romans and wanted to minister there and impart some spiritual gifts to the Roman Christians (Romans 1:11). He also wanted to establish a base of operation from which to go to Spain.

    Paul, by putting himself in the hands of the government, set a pattern for all believers to follow: We are to subject ourselves to the government. The reason is that government is an institution of God. Romans 13:1-6 says, "Let every soul be subject unto the higher powers. For there is no power but of God; the powers that be are ordained of God. Whosoever, therefore, resisteth the power, resisteth the ordinance of God; and they that resist shall receive to themselves judgment. For rulers are not a terror to good works, but to the evil. Wilt thou, then, not be afraid of the power? Do that which is good, and thou shalt have praise of the same; for he is the minister of God to thee for good. But if thou do that which is evil, be afraid; for he beareth not the sword in vain; for he is the minister of God, an avenger to execute wrath upon him that doeth evil. Wherefore, ye must needs be subject, not only for wrath but also for conscience sake. For, for this cause pay ye tribute also; for they are God's ministers, attending continually upon this very thing."

This passage is not saying that every elected official or ruler in the world is a believer; it simply means that government as such is an institution of God. If you fight against the government, you are resisting God. All Christians should be model citizens, not only for their own sakes but lest they receive chastisement from God for not obeying.

Christians are not to be revolutionaries. If the time comes when a government forbids you to love the Lord Jesus Christ or to worship Him, that is a different situation. Normally, we are to be submissive to the laws that exist within the government. Even a bad government will usually protect its citizens and punish criminals. Evil people can do good deeds in the framework of government. As long as Christians obey the government, the government will take care of them.

There is always the possibility of religious persecution; but, generally, if you abide by the law, you will be protected by the government. If you are ticketed for driving one hundred twenty miles an hour in a forty-mile-an-hour zone, don't feel you are being persecuted for righteousness' sake. Romans 13:4 clearly states that governments are ministers of God to effect His will, even at times without their knowledge. If you disobey the government, you have a right to be afraid, "for he beareth not the sword in vain" (v. 4). God gave the government that sword, and the prerogative to do as justice demands. Verse 5 says that the outcome of our obedience is a clear conscience. Verse 6 commands taxes to be paid because, as ministers, government officials are simply collecting the money God has allocated to them.

The Christian then is to subject himself to his government. We are not to be like the Zealots who plundered, used violence, and even killed Jews who obeyed the Roman government. Paul disconnects Christianity from Judaism by making it clear that Christianity and respect for government go together. Civil government, no matter in whose hands it may be, is a divine institution of God. And it is to be obeyed, even if there is a Nero on the throne. The Roman government was ordained of God, so

Paul appealed to a divine institution. Even if a government does not do what it is supposed to do, the standard of obedience is still the same.

3. The Christian's attitude toward persecution

In the early church, there were many people with a martyr complex. They tried hard to die as martyrs because they believed there were two levels of future life: one for normal people and one for martyrs. The man who seeks martyrdom is not a martyr. The only martyr is the one who has fought for every possible escape and found no way out. Paul used every possible resource to avoid death. He didn't initially appeal to Caesar because he knew that might involve death. He waited until the last possible moment for another solution. He was not a spiritual masochist. Some Christians think the only time they are godly is when they're in pain—that the sicker they are, the more holy they must be. But that is not so. If God brings you joy, health, peace, and safety, praise Him. If He brings you pain, thank Him for that as well.

4. The impact of the totally committed life

This one dramatic principle supersedes the others. Only eternity will be able to measure the impact of the apostle Paul. He had a staggering impact on his entire world. I pray to God that I too would maximize whatever impact I could have on this world. The key is to order my priorities, discipline my time, and seek to function within those priorities. Maybe the best way for you to maximize your life is to pour it into three people who will be able to multiply their lives into others (2 Tim. 2:2). Christians ought to realize that one man can affect an entire world if that man is right before God and seeking His glory.

Focusing on the Facts

1. What is the Holy Spirit's purpose in describing Paul on trial in Acts 25:1-12 (see p. 76)?
2. Of what crimes was the apostle Paul accused by the Jewish leaders (Acts 24:5-6; see p. 76)?
3. What was the significance of the city of Caesarea (see p. 77)?
4. Why was it important for Festus to travel to Jerusalem (see p. 77)?
5. What kind of people are most antagonistic toward Christianity (see pp. 77-78)?

6. True or false: Persecution comes as a result of a religious issue (see p. 78).
7. Describe the principle of the power of sin (John 8:30-32; see pp. 78-79).
8. It is clear in the Word of God that nothing happens for_____ unless it is in the framework of God's _____(see p. 80).
9. Describe the patterns of persecution as seen in Matthew 5:11 (see p. 81).
10. Why might Festus have delayed in coming back to Caesarea (Acts 25:6; see p. 82)?
11. According to 1 Peter 3:14-16, what three things is the Christian to do when suffering for the sake of righteousness (see pp. 82-83)?
12. What was one way the Jewish leaders of Paul's day tried to destroy Christianity (see p. 84)?
13. Describe the sect of Judaism known as the Zealots (see p. 84).
14. Christianity is not a _____or a_____ _____but a _____ _____ with the living God (see p. 84).
15. How did the Romans plan to unify the Roman Empire (see p. 84)?
16. According to 1 Peter 2:12-14, what is to be the attitude of the Christian toward the government (see p. 86)?
17. What should have been the logical decision for Festus to make concerning the trials of Paul (see p. 86)?
18. Why did Paul respond so strongly to Festus in Acts 25:10-11 (see p. 86)?
19. What was Paul's right as a Roman citizen (see p. 88)?
20. Did Paul fear the possible judgment of death against him? Support your answer with Scripture (see p. 89).
21. What two courageous things did Paul do in his appeal to Caesar (see p. 89)?
22. Courage is a _____that rightfully belongs to the _____Christian (see p. 90).
23. True or false: Government is an institution designed by God for the effecting of His will (see pp. 90-91).
24. How can you make an impact on your world for Jesus Christ (see p. 91)?

Pondering the Principles

1. Several principles were brought out in the text of Acts 25:1-12, one of which is the power of sin. When a person receives Jesus Christ as Savior and Lord, he is separated from the power and the penalty of sin. One day he will also be separated from sin's

presence. Are you still under the power of sin? If you are, remember that as a Christian, you have the power to say no to sin. Read Romans 6:3-7, and ask God to confirm His sanctifying work in you.

2. Another principle we studied is the exoneration of Christianity. The record stands in the Word of God that no guilty verdict was ever found against the early Christians. Christianity was exonerated by those who had a blameless testimony. Do you have a testimony that validates the truth of Christ in your life? If you were taken to court for being a Christian, would there be enough evidence to convict you? Take time right now to examine your life. Ask God to show that Christianity can be exonerated through your excellent witness.

3. A Christian should be a model citizen toward his government. The reason is that government is an institution of God. The apostle Paul set a pattern for all believers to follow. Are you a model citizen? Do you endeavor to abide by the laws established by your government? Reread Romans 13:1-7, and ask God to reflect what you've learned in this lesson about your attitude toward government.

4. Paul's example demonstrates the impact of the totally dedicated life. There are three keys to developing your dedication to Christ: ordering your priorities, disciplining your time, and seeking to function within the guidelines you've established. If you desire to have an impact like that of the apostle Paul, take the following steps: Order your priorities on a scale from 1-10, discipline yourself daily to achieve those priorities, and seek to function primarily within the areas in which you are gifted. Record your progress daily on paper. Praise God for what you are able to accomplish.

6
Paul Before Agrippa—Part 1
Evaluating the Accusations

Outline

Introduction
A. The Objective
   1. Of Christians in general
   2. Of Paul in specific
B. The Background
   1. Paul's ultimate appeal
      a) To acquire justice
      b) To obey God
   2. Festus's urgent problem
      a) A faultless prisoner
      b) A fortunate intervention

Lesson
I. The Consultation of Paul's Testimony (25:13-22)
   A. Receiving the Royalty (v. 13)
      1. Herod Agrippa II
         a) His family
         b) His fidelity
      2. Bernice
         a) A sister of Agrippa
         b) A symbol of sin
   B. Reviewing the Case (vv. 14-22)
      1. The analysis of the case (v. 14)
      2. The aggravation of the Jews (v. 15)
      3. The avenue of justice (v. 16)
      4. The absence of accusations (vv. 17-18)
      5. The absurdity of the resurrection (v. 19)
      6. The acquiescence of Festus (v. 20)
      7. The appeal of Paul (v. 21)
      8. The anticipation of Agrippa (v. 22)
II. The Circumstances of Paul's Testimony (vv. 23-27)

A. The Contrast Between the Principals (v. 23)
   1. The unsurpassing fantasia (v. 23a)
   2. The unimposing figure (v. 23b)
B. The Content of the Problem (vv. 24-27)
III. The Commencement of Paul's Testimony (26:1-18)
A. Paul's Readiness (v. 1)
   1. The message
   2. The master
B. Paul's Report (vv. 2-18)
   1. His courtesy (vv. 2-3)

Introduction

When I am preaching, my objective is expository. In teaching the Word of God, I try to explain what it means by what it says. I also try to tie each passage into a unit; but I often have trouble getting one unit done at one time. When I approach a passage like Acts 25:13—26:32, I have a difficult time tying it together. It contains quite a few verses—nearly fifty. However, it has to be taken as a unit because the story being told is a unit of thought.

We are looking at historical narrative. We're not examining the proclamation of doctrine; we're looking at the example of Paul and the pattern of his life. The Holy Spirit, for a very explicit reason, has repeatedly given us historical narrative so that we might emulate Paul's actions, not just his words. You should look for two things in this passage: the pattern that Paul used in evangelizing and the boldness of his character. Those appear to be the dominant features of this passage. He was a man who knew no fear and who knew what he wanted to accomplish in the presentation of the gospel.

A. The Objective
   1. Of Christians in general

      Christians are often accused of trying to convert people. That's true; we are definitely trying to convert the unsaved. That is our goal. We are to go into the world to communicate the gospel of Jesus Christ to the unredeemed that they might be redeemed. Some people have said, "Christians are always trying to convert Jews." That's right. Some rabbis have argued that Jews don't try to convert Christians, so why do Christians try to convert the Jews? Because we have this injunction from our Lord Jesus Christ: "Go ye into all the world, and preach the gospel to every creature" (Mark 16:15). That is our objective.

100

2. Of Paul in specific

    We could title Acts 25:13—26:32, "Are you trying to convert me?" because that's exactly what Paul tries to do to King Agrippa. In Acts 26:28 Agrippa tells Paul, "Almost thou persuadest me to be a Christian." I've heard some use that verse to teach that there are many people who are on the verge of coming to Christ. But that is not what it is saying. The Greek text actually says, "Are you with so few words trying to convert me?" Agrippa was mocking Paul. But Paul was trying to convert him and everyone else in the building. Paul's approach in this text is to gain the heart and soul of Agrippa. Paul was a man of objectives, and his goal was to move Agrippa into a position where he could understand the gospel and make an intelligent decision for Christ.

B. The Background

    The apostle Paul had already been proven innocent in four different trials or hearings: before the mob, before the Sanhedrin, before Felix, and before Festus. The thing that stood out in each case was that Paul hadn't done anything. He had not blasphemed God by desecrating the Temple as he was accused. He had not defied Israel by disobeying the Mosaic law. And he had not defied Rome by being an insurrectionist and creating riots against the government. Both the Jewish and Roman courts attested that he had not done those things. But he was retained as a prisoner because the Roman governors didn't have the courage to release him. They knew the Jewish leaders wanted him dead, and they were afraid to let Paul go. They knew they would be pressured—that the Jews would start riots. So both Felix and Festus acquiesced to the leaders' wishes by keeping Paul a prisoner and thereby avoiding their plan to execute him. They knew Paul was innocent. But they were being blackmailed by the Jewish leaders, as many previous Roman governors had been. Paul should have been released, but he remained imprisoned in Caesarea.

1. Paul's ultimate appeal

    a) To acquire justice

        Paul realized that his life was in danger. He knew he wasn't going to get any justice in Caesarea. His last recourse was to take the only option that any Roman citizen could take when brought before any court in the world—he appealed to Caesar (Acts 25:11). He says, in effect, "I can't get any justice here." The Jewish leaders still wanted to kill him. They wanted him to go to Jerusalem so they could ambush him on the way. So Paul made his appeal. In verse 12 Festus says, "Unto Caesar shalt thou go." The only hope Paul had of getting out of trouble was to make his appeal before the court in Rome. That was a bold move because Nero, the emperor at that time, was a murderer. Submitting himself to the judgment of a man like Nero wasn't necessarily a good way out.

b) To obey God

Paul also knew that the Lord had promised him he would make it to Rome (Acts 23:11). The Lord had appeared to him in a cell in Jerusalem and told Paul he would go to Rome and preach the gospel. So Paul anticipated it.

By appealing to Caesar he fulfilled two things: he could be in a place where he would be more likely to receive justice, and he would be in obedience to God's will by going to the place God had designed him to go. Paul had a deep burden to go to Rome. When he wrote his letter to the Romans he said, "I long to see you, that I may impart unto you some spiritual gift" (Rom 1:11). According to Romans 15:24, he wanted to go to them on his way to Spain. In Acts 19:21 he describes plans to go to Jerusalem and then to Rome. Paul thought that if he could make an impact in Rome he could have a great impact on the Roman world. He had no other choice but to appeal his case to Rome, endeavoring to receive justice and follow God's will.

2. Festus's urgent problem

a) A faultless prisoner

When Paul appealed to Rome, Festus had to acquiesce and send him. But Festus had a problem. A report had to accompany the prisoner. This report had to contain the accusations that were brought against the prisoner in the trial. But in Paul's case, there weren't any accusations that carried any weight. So Festus had an innocent prisoner on his hands who had to be sent to Rome and be put on trial. But he didn't have one thing to explain what the trial was about. There was not one thing Paul was guilty of. There weren't any eyewitnesses. The trial took place only because the Jewish leaders wanted Paul dead. They knew he was innocent, but they wanted him dead anyway.

The same thing was true in the case of Jesus. It didn't matter that He was innocent; the Jewish leaders hated Him because He rebuked their sin and unmasked their hypocrisy. They hated Paul for the same reasons. But there was no substantial accusation. So Festus was in a bind—he had to function within the law as a faithful Roman procurator, but he couldn't send a prisoner to Rome along with no accusations.

b)   A fortunate intervention

Fortunately for Festus, King Herod Agrippa II happened to arrive, making a courtesy call on this new procurator. Festus had just been appointed procurator of Judea. Agrippa was the neighboring vassal king. He arrived with his entourage to make a courtesy call on Festus to cement their relationship. Agrippa was the perfect man to help Festus determine an accusation against Paul. Festus thought the reason he couldn't figure out Paul's case was that it was Jewish in nature. When Agrippa, the Jewish king, arrived, he thought he had someone who could untangle his problem.

Lesson

I. THE CONSULTATION OF PAUL'S TESTIMONY (25:13-22)

Agrippa and Festus had a brainstorming session to determine what they were going to do with Paul. Festus had to come up with some accusation, and he needed Agrippa to help him.

A.   Receiving the Royalty (v. 13)

"After certain days King Agrippa and Bernice came unto Caesarea to greet Festus."

1.   Herod Agrippa II

Festus was the superior to Herod. Even though Herod was king, he was only a vassal king. The Roman government had subjugated all Israel's authority, and Herod was nothing but a puppet king. In fact, He was reared for most of his life in Rome. It wasn't until his father died and he was given some territory to rule in Israel that he left Rome. And he spent the last days of his life in Rome. He was Roman in allegiance although he was part Jewish. As king he was in charge of the appointment of priests and the operation of the ceremonies of Jewish worship. So he was very familiar with the Jewish religion.

a) His family

Agrippa was one of the Herods. The Herodian family was a family of kings. They dominated the rulership of the New Testament era. The rulers began with Herod the Great and extended to Herod Agrippa II. He was the last of the Herods. Herod Agrippa II was the brother of Bernice. They had one of the most infamous relationships in all history because they lived in incest. Interestingly, Bernice was also the sister of Drusilla, the wife of Felix, who was the governor before Festus. Herod Agrippa II was the son of Herod Agrippa I, who had James beheaded and Peter imprisoned. According to Acts 12:21, he decided to have a day for himself in Caesarea. As he made a proclamation, the people said, "It is the voice of a god, and not of a man. And immediately an angel of the Lord smote him . . . and he was eaten of worms and died" (Acts 12:22-23). That's how Herod Agrippa II's father died. Herod Agrippa II's great uncle, Herod Antipas, beheaded John the Baptist. And his great grandfather, Herod the Great, killed all the babies in Bethlehem (Matt. 2:16). Agrippa II belonged to a disastrous family.

b) His fidelity

It was proper for a Jewish king to pay a courtesy call on a new procurator. Agrippa was very accommodating to Rome. He had been reared in Rome and lived there until his father died in A.D. 44. Claudius, the emperor of Rome, wanted to appoint him to his father's kingdom, but Agrippa was only seventeen. Claudius waited another six years until Agrippa was twenty-three and gave him a part of the territory. Later, when he was twenty-seven, they gave him a little more. But Agrippa never ruled more than a relatively small area of Northern Palestine and

Galilee. He was strictly a vassal king. He established his capital at Caesarea Philippi, a different Caesarea than the one on the coast of the Mediteranean. This city was located to the north. Agrippa had its name changed to Neronius to flatter Nero.

During the Jewish war, which brought on the destruction of Jerusalem in A.D. 70, he tried to prevent the Jews from revolting. But when Vespasian moved his troops against Jerusalem, he joined the Roman army and fought against the Jews. He was a traitor to Judaism. He eventually died in Rome, the last of the Herodian dynasty.

2. Bernice

   a) A sister of Agrippa

   Bernice was Agrippa's sister. Josephus, the major historian of that era, said that they lived in incest (*Antiquities* 20.7.3). It was common knowledge. Every so often she would have an interlude with a lover but would come back to Agrippa. In fact, Vespasian's son Titus, who was instrumental in the destruction of Jerusalem, took Bernice as his lover. When he took her to Rome, the gossip about her became so bad that he left her. But she went right back to Agrippa. They continued that relationship the rest of their lives.

   b) A symbol of sin

   Acts 25:13 says, "After certain days King Agrippa and Bernice." Verse 23 says, "And on the next day, when Agrippa was come, and Bernice." Then Acts 26:30 says, "When he had thus spoken, the king rose up, and the governor, and Bernice." Bernice wasn't left out of anything. Why would the Holy Spirit keep adding the phrase "and Bernice"? I think the Holy Spirit is pinpointing something important. She is attached to Agrippa like an ugly disease. She is the symbol of his vice. There are two words that characterize Agrippa: "And Bernice." Every time that man appears, Bernice is with him. Dr. H. A. Ironside said, "If Agrippa died unsaved, we may be sure God links Bernice with him still; and when Agrippa stands eventually at the judgment of the Great White Throne, Bernice will stand there with him! In other words, Bernice represents that sin, that evil thing in the life of a man and woman from which they can never be separated either in time or in eternity—if they do not judge the sin and get right before God. . . . Surely there is something intensely solemn here! Oh, the awfulness of sin! How it clings to one!" (*Lectures on the Book of Acts* [N.J.: Loizeaux, 1975], pp. 594-95). That's a vivid illustration.

Agrippa was decadent and immoral and the descendant of an infamous family. But he did know about Judaism, and Festus needed to learn some things about Judaism. So Agrippa was a welcome guest. Apparently Agrippa had a good reputation in Jewish matters because the apostle Paul acknowledged him as an expert in Acts 26:3.

B. Reviewing the Case (vv. 14-22)

1. The analysis of the case (v. 14)

"And when they had been there many days, Festus declared Paul's cause unto the king, saying, There is a certain man left in bonds by Felix."

Finally, the right time came, and Festus told Agrippa that Felix left a certain man in prison when he was recalled by Rome. Festus began to review for Herod the situation regarding Paul. Remember Acts 24:27 says that Felix left him in prison to do a favor for the Jews. That's the only reason Paul was still in prison. He was innocent.

2. The aggravation of the Jews (v. 15)

"About whom, when I was at Jerusalem, the chief priests and the elders of the Jews informed me, desiring to have judgment against him."

After spending a few days at Caesarea when he was inducted into the governorship, Festus immediately went to Jerusalem to try to develop some kind of relationship with the religious leaders. But as soon as he arrived, the chief priests and elders informed him that they wanted Paul to be condemned. They did not want a trial; they just wanted an execution. Festus was in a bad spot because he didn't know why they wanted him dead or why Felix left him in bonds.

3. The avenue of justice (v. 16)

"To whom I answered, It is not the manner of the Romans to deliver any man to die, before he who is accused have the accusers face to face, and have opportunity to answer for himself concerning the accusation laid against him."

Roman law prohibited the execution of a man without a trial. We have inherited that concept today. We have a legal system that allows the accused to face his accusers. All the evidence must be detailed and a verdict determined. That's what Roman justice demanded. The case had to come to a resolution before a sentence could be passed. On the basis of Roman justice, Festus couldn't honor the demand of the Jewish leaders. But they planned to blackmail Festus. If he wanted to have a successful rulership, he would have to honor their request. But Festus didn't allow them to do that at the beginning. Since Roman law demanded a trial, he told them to come to Caesarea for an official trial.

4. The absence of accusations (vv. 17-18)

"Therefore, when they were come here, without any delay on the next day I sat on the judgment seat, and commanded the man to be brought forth; against whom, when the accusers stood up, they brought no accusation of such things as I [had continually] supposed."

Festus had probably manufactured some idea of what Paul had done. Claudius Lysias had done the same thing, supposing Paul to be an Egyptian rebel (Acts 21:38). I'm sure Felix had his ideas about who Paul was also. I'm sure Festus thought Paul had done something wrong, but the Jewish leaders didn't bring any accusations against him. That's why Festus had a problem. He had inherited an innocent man from Felix. He knew the leaders wanted him dead, but he couldn't figure out what Paul had done wrong. To make matters worse for Festus, Paul appealed to Caesar. So he had to send him to Rome, but he didn't have one thing to report.

5. The absurdity of the resurrection (v. 19)

"[The Jews] had certain questions against him of their own religion, and of one Jesus, who was dead, whom Paul affirmed to be alive."

After seeing that no criminal accusation was brought against Paul, Festus discovered that the case centered on an argument about religion. All he could determine was that Paul was saying a dead man by the name of Jesus was alive. Festus thought Paul was out of his mind. He couldn't understand why the Jewish leaders would bother with him. Intelligent Romans knew that people didn't rise from the dead. To Festus, if Paul wanted to affirm that Jesus was alive, then he ought to be left alone because no one would believe him anyway. But Festus didn't understand the implications of the resurrection because he didn't understand the implications of the Messiah. He didn't understand the life and work of Jesus Christ. He didn't even know who Jesus was. And we can't expect Festus to understand. He was trapped in his ignorance. But he did become informed about the resurrection. No matter the situation, Paul always communicated the central issue—that Jesus is not dead but alive. And we believe He is alive.

Festus badly needed Agrippa's help. He didn't even know why a trial was necessary. But Paul appealed to Rome, and if they were going to send him there, they would need some kind of accusation.

6. The acquiescence of Festus (v. 20)

"And because I was perplexed concerning such manner of questions, I asked him whether he would go to Jerusalem, and there be judged of these matters."

Festus told Agrippa he was confused about some of the facts and suggested that they go to Jerusalem. The truth is that the Jewish leaders were pressuring him to go to Jerusalem so they could ambush and kill Paul on the journey (Acts 25:3). But Festus wanted to look good in front of Agrippa, so he lied and said that he had determined to take Paul to Jerusalem for his own sake.

7. The appeal of Paul (v. 21)

"But when Paul had appealed to be reserved unto the hearing of Augustus, I commanded him to be kept till I might send him to Caesar."

Once Paul heard that he was going to Jerusalem, he appealed to Caesar. He knew that if he didn't receive justice in Caesarea, he was sure not to get it in Jerusalem. Paul took the route that every Roman citizen had. If he couldn't get justice where he was, he could appeal to Rome.

Verse 21 says that Paul appealed to "Augustus." That was not the current Caesar's name. *Augustus* is an adjective. The name *Augustus Caesar* is not a proper name for

Caesar; it was an adjective for all the Caesars. When we say there was an august body, we are referring to a meeting of dignified individuals. The word for "Augustus" in the Greek text is *sebastos*. It comes from a root word that means "to worship." So Augustus means "the worshiped one" or "the revered one." Who was the revered one? The Augustus Caesar of that day was Nero, who could be properly called Augustus Caesar Nero. The term *Augustus* was first applied to Octavian, the first Roman emperor. It was then applied to each Caesar in succession. Paul wanted to see the revered and honorable Caesar.

Once Paul made the appeal, Festus had no choice—he commanded Paul to be retained in Caesarea until he could send him to Rome. But he couldn't send him because he didn't know what to tell Rome about him. He couldn't tell them that Paul was mad, claiming that someone was alive who was really dead. Rome wouldn't have been interested.

8. The anticipation of Agrippa (v. 22)

"Then Agrippa said unto Festus, I would also hear the man myself. Tomorrow, said he, thou shalt hear him."

The phrase "I would also hear the man myself" is in the imperfect tense. It gives the idea of a continuous action. Agrippa may have been continually wanting to hear from Paul himself, having already heard about him. Paul was a curiosity for Agrippa.

II. THE CIRCUMSTANCES OF PAUL'S TESTIMONY (vv. 23-27)

A. The Contrast Between the Principals (v. 23)

1. The unsurpassing fantasia (v. 23*a*)

"And on the next day, when Agrippa was come, and Bernice, with great pomp."

Fantasia is the Greek word that is translated in verse 23 as "pomp." Agrippa appeared with his entire entourage with great pomp. You can imagine Agrippa and Bernice dressed in purple robes. The soldiers that served as a ceremonial guard would have been in their best uniforms. And all the important dignitaries would have been there.

2. The unimposing figure (v. 23b)

"[When they] entered into the place of hearing [the auditorium], with the chief captains, and principal men of the city, at Festus' commandment Paul was brought forth."

If we can believe tradition, Paul was not very imposing physically. With all the glitter in the auditorium, in walked a little bandy-legged, bald-headed Jewish man who might not have seen too well. He was shackled by a chain as he stood in the middle of the auditorium. You can imagine people saying, "Did we come to hear him?" But it didn't matter what was going on around Paul because he always dominated the scene. Luke, the writer of Acts, displayed his great sense of humor in contrasting Paul with those in attendance. Agrippa, Bernice, and Festus were the fools putting on a big show, while Paul stood as the hero of the scene.

B. The Content of the Problem (vv. 24-27)

"Festus said, King Agrippa, and all men who are here present with us, ye see this man, about whom all the multitude of the Jews have dealt with me, both at Jerusalem, and also here, crying that he ought not to live any longer. But when I found that he had committed nothing worthy of death, and that he himself hath appealed to Augustus, I have determined to send him; of whom I have no certain thing to write unto my lord. Wherefore, I have brought him forth before you, and specially before thee, O King Agrippa, that, after examination, I might have somewhat to write. For it seemeth to me unreasonable to send a prisoner and not signify the accusations laid against him."

Festus was very open and honest about his problem. He couldn't send Paul to Rome without an accusation, so he turned his problem over to Agrippa. This wasn't an official trial but merely a hearing to satisfy Agrippa's curiosity and to find an accusation that Festus could put in his report to Rome.

Paul didn't have to show up at the hearing. He ultimately would have been dragged in, but he didn't have to appear legally. He could have argued wisely from the law and said, "You can't take me in there. I've had my trial. I've been judged innocent, and I pleaded my case to Rome." He might have been able to get out of it, but Paul didn't even try. Why wouldn't he want to get out of it? Because it was another platform for him to preach Christ. He turned everything that ever happened to him into an opportunity to preach Christ.

What a beautiful setting Paul had for preaching! The place was jammed with people who didn't know the Lord, and he had them all as an audience. The objective of the church is to go into the world and preach the gospel. The church meets to pray, break bread together, fellowship, and study the Word of God, but it never meets to evangelize—it has to go out into the world to do that. Paul was confronting the world. He was surrounded by a Roman entourage and all the Jewish dignitaries of that part of the world. He was as bold and fearless as any man who ever lived. His testimony was fantastic. His presentation was dynamic and penetrating as he unmasked the sin of those present.

III. THE COMMENCEMENT OF PAUL'S TESTIMONY (26:1-18)

A. Paul's Readiness (v. 1)

"Then Agrippa said unto Paul, Thou art permitted to speak for thyself. Then Paul stretched forth the hand, and answered for himself."

1. The message

   Paul answered for himself. That's what Peter meant when he said, "Be ready always to give an answer to every man that asketh you a reason of the hope that is in you, with meekness and fear" (1 Pet. 3:15). When we confront people with the claims of Christ and try to convert them, we need to know the right information. Paul said, "Be instant in season, out of season" (2 Tim. 4:2, KJV*). Being instant means that you have the information. We ought to have a reservoir of knowledge of the Word of God. We must be ready to give an answer to the one who asks the reason for the hope that is in us.

2. The master

   The Lord Jesus Christ was a master of turning every opportunity to Himself in a way that none of us can duplicate. A woman at a well needed water. Christ told her that He was the water of life and that she could have a well of water in her springing up to eternal life (John 4:14). Many people needed food, so He fed them bread and said, "I am the bread of life" (John 6:35). A great candelabra was in the middle of the Temple when Jesus

King James Version.

walked in and said, "I am the light of the world" (John 8:12). A high priest poured water out of a pitcher while the people thanked God. Jesus then said, "If any man thirst, let him come unto me, and drink" (John 7:37). Jesus was the master of turning every occasion to Himself. Paul drank deeply of that very same spirit. In case after case, the circumstances became the platform for his proclamation.

You need to think like Jesus and Paul. One of the characteristics of successful evangelism is the ability to turn your circumstances into an opportunity to present the gospel and magnify the Lord Jesus Christ. How is that accomplished? By being ready and anxious to do it. It is really a question of boldness, not method. You can learn all the methods in the world on how to win people to the Lord, but nothing will happen if you're not walking in the Spirit and allowing Him to move your heart to be bold enough to speak. The apostle Paul was ready to speak. He had been waiting two years to say something, and now he had his opportunity.

Two Testimonies

Martin Niemöller was a German pastor who was arrested by the Nazis and spent nine years in prison. At the end of World War II, he came to America when he was released. There was much interest in his arrival, so he traveled across America and spoke about the horrors of nine years in a Nazi prison. Two reporters commented on Niemöller and his speech in one city: "Imagine," said one reporter disgustedly, "nine years in a Nazi prison and all he can talk about is Jesus Christ!" Isn't that a great testimony? Paul spent only two years in confinement in Caesarea, and all he could talk about was Jesus Christ. Paul's testimony was always about Jesus Christ.

There was a man of God who was a great soul winner. Someone asked him what made him so fruitful in winning people to Christ. He said, "One day I prayed a prayer that changed my life. I asked God to give me the opportunity, that every time I'm able to introduce the topic of conversation, it would always be Jesus Christ." That's what changed his life. God only knows how many people he won to Jesus Christ.

Paul talked about Jesus Christ. Two years of imprisonment hadn't paled his desire to speak. I'm sure as he looked at Agrippa, his heart grieved. Paul had the love of God toward that man and wanted him to hear the gospel. Paul was about to speak to

Agrippa concerning Jesus Christ. He was going to testify about Jesus being alive from the dead—the thing he said over and over. Wouldn't it be great if the world said of us, "Did you know those people keep saying that Jesus is alive?" Wouldn't it be great to have that reputation?

B. Paul's Report (vv. 2-18)

1. His courtesy (vv. 2-3)

"I think myself happy, King Agrippa, because I shall answer for myself this day before thee concerning all the things of which I am accused of the Jews, especially because I know thee to be expert in all customs and questions which are among the Jews; wherefore, I beseech thee to hear me patiently."

As a matter of courtesy, Paul addressed Agrippa, the key figure in the room, but he knew everyone else was going to listen. And they were especially going to listen when they knew he was addressing the king. Two men stand in confrontation—one stands a prisoner, the other sits a king. But the one is an enslaved king and the other an enthroned prisoner. Paul's heart desired the conversion of Agrippa. When Paul ends his testimony in Acts 26:28, Agrippa in effect says, "Are you trying to convert me?" That's exactly what Paul was trying to do—not only Agrippa but everyone else as well. Acts 26:4 begins one of the supreme defenses of the Christian faith. And it began with a courteous approach to Agrippa.

Paul's testimony was not so much a defense of the Christian faith as it was a proclamation. When you are drawn before the tribunals of the world, your purpose is not to defend yourself but to win people to Jesus Christ. That is always our purpose. Paul didn't complain about his circumstances; he presented the gospel. Paul must have thought that Agrippa would be open to the gospel. Agrippa would have understood Paul's logic and reasoning because he understood the Jewish situation and customs. But at the same time he wouldn't be sympathetic to the Sanhedrin because of his allegiance to Rome. So Paul thought he had an objective listener—one who was objective as a Roman yet oriented toward Judaism. Agrippa might have been a potential convert. Paul also realized the influence Agrippa would have if he became a believer. Was Paul trying to convert Agrippa? Absolutely. As Christians, we try to convert everyone we can.

Focusing on the Facts

1. What two dominant features about Paul can one find in Acts 25:13—26:32 (see p. 96)?
2. What is the objective of a Christian (Mark 16:15; see p. 96)?
3. Why was Paul kept as a prisoner when he had been proven innocent (see p. 97)?
4. Why did Paul appeal his case to Caesar (see pp. 97-98)?
5. Why did Paul want to take the gospel to Rome (see p. 98)?
6. Explain the problem Festus had when Paul appealed his case to Caesar (see pp. 98-99).
7. Why did Festus think that Agrippa was the perfect man to solve his problem (see p. 99)?
8. Why did Agrippa have knowledge of Jewish religious worship (see p. 100)?
9. Describe Agrippa's relationship with Rome (see pp. 100-101).
10. What is significant about Bernice's attachment to Agrippa (see pp. 101-2)?
11. Why couldn't Festus honor the Jewish leaders' demand to have Paul executed (Acts 25:16; see pp. 102-3)?
12. Why did Festus decide to take Paul back to Jerusalem (Acts 25:20; see p. 104)?
13. Explain the meaning of "Augustus" (Acts 25:21; see pp. 104-5).
14. Why didn't Paul have to appear at the hearing before Agrippa? Why did he appear (see p. 106)?
15. What makes evangelism different from other ministries that the church carries out (see p. 107)?
16. What should every Christian do before he confronts unbelievers with the claims of Christ (1 Pet. 3:15; see p. 107)?
17. Give some examples of how Jesus turned everyday situations into opportunities to proclaim Himself (see pp. 107-8).
18. What is more important in evangelism, the method or the boldness on the part of the presenter? Explain your answer (see p. 108).
19. What is the purpose for every Christian brought before the tribunals of the world (see p. 109)?

Pondering the Principles

1. When Paul made his appeal to Caesar, he took advantage of a right he had as a Roman citizen. Have you ever thought about how fortunate it was for Paul that he was a Roman citizen? But he

was more than fortunate, because God used his citizenship to create inroads for the gospel in many new areas around the world. A Jew like Peter wouldn't have had the same access. What about you? Has God used you in certain ministries that have taken advantage of your background or experiences? If He has, then you have seen God's sovereign plan at work. Thank Him for the design He has for your life. Thank Him not only for the way He has gifted you but also for the experiences He has brought you through, even if some of them occurred while you were an unbeliever. Remember, every aspect of your life has fallen within the divine plan of God. Praise Him for that.

2. What happens when you are faced with an opportunity to proclaim Christ to someone? Do you take advantage of the opportunity, or do you let it slip away? But we have a greater calling than to just take advantage of the opportunities presented to us, for we should be seeking to create opportunities to share Christ also. We need to have the perspective of the man of God who wanted to include Jesus Christ in every conversation (see p. 108). Paul didn't have to appear before Agrippa, but he did so he could share Christ with him. Beginning today, seek opportunities to share Christ. Ask God to give you His discernment so you can know when you should share the gospel. When the opportunity comes, be bold in your presentation. Remember that the Holy Spirit will give you that boldness.

7

Paul Before Agrippa—Part 2
The Commencement of Paul's Testimony

Outline

Introduction
A. Reviewing the Historical Context
B. Reaffirming the Christian Commission
   1. Paul's passion
      a) The theological base
         (1) The motivation
         (2) The ministry
         (3) The method
         (4) The moment
      b) The practical business
   2. Paul's commission

Review
  I. The Consultation of Paul's Testimony (25:13-22)
 II. The Circumstances of Paul's Testimony (25:23-27)
III. The Commencement of Paul's Testimony (26:1-18)
   A. Paul's Readiness (v. 1)
   B. Paul's Report (vv. 2-18)
     1. His courtesy (vv. 2-3)

Lesson
     2. His conduct (vv. 4-5)
       a) Paul's experience
       b) Paul's emphasis
     3. His condemnation (vv. 6-8)
       a) The revelation of the hope (v. 6)
       b) The representatives of the hope (v. 7*a*)
       c) The rejection of the hope (vv. 7*b*-8)
         (1) By Agrippa
         (2) By the Jewish leaders
     4. His confession (vv. 9-11)
       a) Paul fought against Christ (v. 9)

      b) Paul imprisoned Christians (v. 10)
      c) Paul persecuted Christians (v. 11)
  5. His conversion (vv. 12-15)
      a) Fighting a losing battle (vv. 12-14)
      b) Submitting to Christ's lordship (v. 15)
  6. His commission (vv. 16-18)
      a) Paul's calling (vv. 16-17)
         (1) As an apostle
            (*a*) Appointed by the Lord
            (*b*) An eyewitness of the resurrection
         (2) As a minister
      b) His message (v. 18)
         (1) Conviction
         (2) Illumination
            (*a*) Living in darkness
            (*b*) Living in light
         (3) Conversion
         (4) Pardon
            (*a*) 1 John 2:12
            (*b*) Romans 4:8
            (*c*) Romans 8:33-34
         (5) Inheritance
         (6) Faith

Introduction

A good title for Acts 25:13—26:32 would be "Are you trying to convert me?" In Acts 26:28, after Paul finished his testimony, King Agrippa II says in effect, "Do you think that in such a short time you can persuade me to be a Christian? Are you, with so few words, trying to convert me?" Of course that's exactly what the apostle Paul was trying to do. And he was trying to convert not only Agrippa but also everyone else in the auditorium.

A. Reviewing the Historical Context

    Paul was repeatedly called to answer accusations brought against him by the Jewish leaders. He was accused of sedition—of stirring up trouble against Rome. He was accused of sectarianism—of being a Jewish religious heretic. And he was accused of sacrilege—of blaspheming God by desecrating the Temple. But he didn't do any of those things. He was totally exonerated on all counts by all courts because there was no evidence or eyewitnesses.

    Although Paul was innocent, he remained a prisoner. The

reason is simple. Felix knew Paul was innocent, but he wouldn't let him go because that would upset the Jewish leaders and the political applecart in Judea. When Festus took over the governorship, Paul was still in custody. But he didn't want to release him because he didn't want to upset the Jews either. Both governors had been blackmailed into keeping Paul a prisoner.

When Paul appealed to Rome, Festus had another problem. Since Paul couldn't get any justice in Caesarea, he decided to do what all Roman citizens had the right to do: Appeal to Caesar so his case would be transferred to Rome. But Festus couldn't send Paul to Rome without a written accusation. And he couldn't find anything to accuse Paul of. In the midst of his dilemma, King Herod Agrippa II arrived to pay a courtesy call on Festus. At that point, Festus saw a possible way out of his dilemma. He thought that if he could get Agrippa to listen to Paul, Agrippa might come up with some viable accusation to justify the trial in Rome. Then Festus could maintain a balance with the Jewish leaders.

B. Reaffirming the Christian Commission

The thing that stands out in Paul's testimony to Agrippa is not so much the defense Paul gives as his effort to convert Agrippa to Christianity. He attempts to get Agrippa to respond to the gospel. Paul even extends an invitation to him at the end of his testimony. Now, Paul didn't have to appear at this hearing because legally his appeal to Rome had to be honored. But I believe he appeared because he saw it as an opportunity to preach the gospel. Festus looked at it as an opportunity to get an accusation. Agrippa looked at it as a curiosity—he wanted to hear Paul. So Paul's testimony took place in the Roman praetorium in Caesarea before King Agrippa, Bernice, and all their entourage, before Festus and all the chief captains, and before all the famous people in the city of Caesarea.

1. Paul's passion

As we look at Paul's testimony, we can't help but be reminded of the one great passion of Paul: preaching the gospel. His own security didn't matter to him. It didn't matter if he was embarrassed or if people thought he was strange. It didn't matter if they thought he was crazy. It didn't matter if they put him in chains, in jail, or killed him. Boldness is the result of realizing that you are expendable for the cause of Christ. Paul believed that.

a) The theological base

Second Corinthians 5:17—6:2 forms the base of theology on which Paul operated in Acts 25 and 26.

(1) The motivation

In 2 Corinthians 5:17 Paul says, "If any man be in Christ, he is a new creation; old things are passed away; behold, all things are become new." Paul believed that the gospel transformed men. That became Paul's motivation in preaching. When you have confidence in something, you tend to be motivated by it. Paul believed in what the gospel could accomplish; therefore, he was motivated by it. It's hard to promote something you don't believe in. Paul believed in the transforming power of the gospel, and that was the basis of his desire to proclaim it.

(2) The ministry

Verse 18 says, "All things are of God, who hath reconciled us to himself by Jesus Christ, and hath given to us the ministry of reconciliation." The word *reconciled* means "to bring back into proper adjustment." The New Testament uses it only of men, never of God. He doesn't need to be reconciled because He's never out of adjustment. Some people think that God is reconciled to man. No, it is man who must be brought back into proper adjustment to God. That's the ministry of reconciliation. The Bible tells us that we have been given the ministry of bringing people into proper adjustment to God. We are in the business of converting maladjusted, anti-God people into well-adjusted, God-oriented people. We are trying to bring men to the place where they can become a new creation in Christ, with old things passing away and all things becoming new.

Verse 19 says, "God was in Christ reconciling the world unto himself, not imputing their trespasses unto them, and hath committed unto us the word of reconciliation." God has given us the gospel message, which is the word of reconciliation. We are to carry it to the world, which is the ministry of reconciliation. We are ambassadors (v. 20). An ambassador is someone who represents his own government in a foreign land. We represent the government of God in a foreign land.

(3) The method

What does an ambassador do? What does the ministry of reconciliation involve? Verse 20 says, "As though God did beseech you by us; we beg you in Christ's stead, be ye reconciled to God." We must be engaged in a driving, compassionate activity. We are to beg people to be converted. We are to plead with them. There is nothing wrong with begging people to come to Christ. We are to beg them to be reconciled to God—to be rightly adjusted to Him. We need to be committed to the ministry of reconciliation.

(4) The moment

There must be a tremendous sense of urgency connected with this ministry. Second Corinthians 6:1-2 says, "We, then, as workers together with him, beseech you also that ye receive not the grace of God in vain (for he saith, I have heard thee in a time accepted, and in the day of salvation have I helped thee; behold, now is the accepted time; behold, now is the day of salvation)."

Paul tells us that we've been granted the word of reconciliation—the good news of how people can be properly adjusted with God. We also have been given the ministry of reconciliation, which means carrying that good news to the world. And there is to be an urgency about it—today is the day it must be done.

b) The practical business

We have been placed into this world to bring maladjusted men into adjustment with God, and that involves conversion. When Agrippa asked Paul if he was trying to convert him (Acts 26:28), he put his finger on the goal and objective of every believer who confronts an unbeliever. We are in the business of converting people in the power of the Holy Spirit. We can become so complacent in our sanctification, so happy in our fellowship, and so blessed with what is happening in the Christian community that we forget about a world full of people who are going to hell. We must keep them in perspective. In Mark 16:15 our Lord lays down this simple commission: "Go ye into all the world, and preach the gospel to every creature." In Luke 24:46-48 He says, "Thus it is written, and thus it behooved Christ to suffer, and to rise from the dead the third day; and that repentance and remission [forgiveness] of sins should be preached in his name among all nations, beginning at Jerusalem. And ye are witnesses of these things." The commission is clear.

2. Paul's commission

    Paul understood his calling from the first day of his conversion. In Acts 26:16-18 Paul tells us what the Lord said to him, "Rise, and stand upon thy feet; for I have appeared unto thee for this purpose, to make thee a minister and a witness both of these things which thou hast seen, and of those things in which I will appear unto thee; delivering thee from the people, and from the Gentiles, unto whom now I send thee, to open their eyes, and to turn them from darkness to light, and from the power of Satan unto God." Paul knew that the Lord had given him the ministry of turning people from darkness to light and from Satan to God. It was a commitment to convert people. Notice verse 17: "Delivering thee from the people [the Jews], and from the Gentiles, unto whom now I send thee." When God saved you, He took you out of the world to send you back into the world.

Have You Become Too Satisfied?

I fear that we as Christians can become so satisfied with learning, fellowship, unity, and growth, that we forget we have been taken out of the world to be sent back into the world to transform people in the energy of the Holy Spirit. That is the gospel commission.

1. Ephesians 6:19-20—The apostle Paul told the Ephesians to pray "for me, that utterance may be given unto me, that I may open my mouth boldly to make known the mystery of the gospel, for which I am an ambassador in bonds; that in this I may speak boldly, as I ought to speak." That's a prayer we ought to pray for each other.

2. 2 Timothy 4:5—Paul said, "Do the work of an evangelist,

make full proof of thy ministry." He was saying that for Timothy to make full proof of the ministry, he would have to do some evangelizing. I remember a young man who said to me, "I don't think I have the gift of evangelism." I told him that no one has the gift of evangelism; we just have the command. It isn't an isolated gift; it's something that all of us should do. We are to change people. If someone asks if you are trying to convert them, tell them you are. That's our calling. And I trust that we're doing it in a loving way.

Paul's task was clear. He was given the opportunity to preach the gospel before many significant people in Caesarea. And he seized that opportunity—the marvelous privilege that the Spirit of God gave him. Paul's testimony provided entertainment for Agrippa, grounds of accusation for Festus, and a tremendous opportunity to proclaim the gospel for Paul

Review

I. THE CONSULTATION OF PAUL'S TESTIMONY (25:13-22; see pp. 99-105)

II. THE CIRCUMSTANCES OF PAUL'S TESTIMONY (25:23-27; see pp. 105-7)

III. THE COMMENCEMENT OF PAUL'S TESTIMONY (26:1-18)

A. Paul's Readiness (v. 1; see pp. 107-9)

"Then Agrippa said unto Paul, Thou art permitted to speak for thyself. Then Paul stretched forth the hand, and answered for himself."

B. Paul's Report (vv. 2-18)

1. His courtesy (vv. 2-3; see p. 109)

"I think myself happy, King Agrippa, because I shall answer for myself this day before thee concerning all the things of which I am accused of the Jews, especially because I know thee to be expert in all customs and questions which are among the Jews; wherefore, I beseech thee to hear me patiently."

I believe Paul thought Agrippa would be objective. The Jerusalem leaders were biased against and hateful of Rome. But Agrippa was part Jewish and had been educated in Rome. His total allegiance was toward Rome. He played politics in Israel, but deep in his heart he was a Roman. Given that background, Paul thought that Agrippa would understand the character of his argument. He also thought Agrippa would be more objective in evaluating it. He wouldn't be swayed by the terrible Jewish hatred of Jesus Christ. So Paul thought there was a good chance that Agrippa might have his life changed. A person with an open heart would hear the gospel, so Paul used the opportunity to try to convert Agrippa.

Paul's testimony was centered on this: Christ is the Messiah as proven by His resurrection. And Christ's resurrection is proven by Paul's transformed life. So Paul's testimony follows the events of his transformation when he met Christ on the road to Damascus. In effect, Paul is saying, "I couldn't argue when the Lord Jesus Christ, alive from the dead, struck me down on the road to Damascus, changed my life, and commissioned me into the ministry. He has to be the Messiah; He has to be the Savior." That is Paul's argument.

Paul wanted to give his testimony because he wanted the people in that auditorium to see the change that Christ had made in his life. One of the great proofs of Christianity is a transformed life. In 2 Corinthians 5:17 Paul says, "If any man be in Christ, he is a new creation." That is one of the great motives of evangelism. And one of the great testimonies of the gospel is a changed life. Paul wanted Agrippa to know what Jesus did in his life. Agrippa didn't need to hear the facts of the gospel—he already knew them (v. 26)—but he did need to hear what Christ had done in His resurrection power.

Lesson

2. His conduct (vv. 4-5)

"My manner of life from my youth, which was at the first among mine own nation at Jerusalem, know all the Jews, who knew me from the beginning, if they would testify, that after the strictest sect of our religion I lived a Pharisee."

a) Paul's experience

From the earliest years of his life, Paul was educated at Jerusalem. If the Jewish leaders had the courage to

124

testify, they would admit that he had belonged to the strictest sect of their religion, the Pharisees. A Pharisee was a strict legalist. And Paul was at the strictest end—he was a right-wing Pharisee. From his youth he was trained in orthodox Judaism in Jerusalem. The Jewish leaders knew he had sat at the feet of Gamaliel, a chief rabbi.

b) Paul's emphasis

In verse 5, Paul does something in using the word translated "strictest," which Greek writers and speakers are allowed to do but which we're not allowed to do in English: He uses a double superlative. That puts heavy emphasis on "strictest" in the Greek text. Paul is saying that he belonged to the most strictest sect. He stresses that if anyone ever lived who was convinced that Judaism was the final word from God, it was he. He belonged to the most extreme legal view. And everyone knew it. Paul was setting his audience up for the account of his transformation. He wanted to show them his zealousness as a Jew so they might understand the tremendous, cataclysmic effect of the transformation that took place in him.

3. His condemnation (vv. 6-8)

a) The revelation of the hope (v. 6)

"And now I stand and am judged for the hope of the promise made of God unto our fathers."

Paul was raised a Jew, had been a Pharisee, and now was being condemned for believing in the promise God made to the Jewish fathers. What promise? Verse 6 says it is "the hope of the promise." What was the Jewish hope? It was the coming of Messiah. The hope of every Jew was that Messiah would come and deliver Israel. The nation of Israel had been struggling against bondage from the days in Egypt right up to the time under Rome. They had had some years of independence and some years of success under David, but for the most part, they knew nothing but fighting, struggling, and slavery. Since 586 B.C. they had known abject slavery under various world powers, such as the Babylonians, Persians, Greeks, and now the Romans. They longed for the Messiah to come. They believed that when He did come, He would set up His kingdom, and that the dead Jews would be resurrected to enjoy it. That was the Jewish hope.

Job 19:26-27 says, "Though after my skin worms destroy this body, yet in my flesh shall I see God: whom I shall see for myself, and mine eyes shall behold, and not another; though my reigns be consumed within me" (KJV). The Jewish people knew all along there would be a resurrection. The resurrection was their hope that the Messiah would deliver Israel, set up His kingdom, and raise the dead Jews to enjoy the kingdom. And that is going to happen. So Paul says he was being condemned for believing what Jewish people have believed throughout history.

b) The representatives of the hope (v. 7a)

"Unto which promise our twelve tribes, earnestly serving God day and night, hope to come."

Paul didn't invent the hope; all twelve tribes agreed to it. By the way, Paul didn't believe there were only two tribes, and the other ten were lost. Paul indicates that the twelve tribes were still together. That's what the Bible teaches. Before the ten tribes were taken away by the Assyrians, individual members filtered into the two tribes in the south. The two tribes became a composite of all twelve. So Paul says that the twelve tribes still earnestly hoped for the coming of Messiah.

c) The rejection of the hope (vv. 7b-8)

"For which hope's sake, King Agrippa, I am accused by the Jews. Why should it be thought a thing incredible with you, that God should raise the dead?"

Agrippa couldn't have had a problem with God raising the dead because that's what most Jews believed. Paul wanted to know why he had to suffer abuse and condemnation for simply believing in the resurrection. That was not an incredible belief. The Pharisees couldn't argue against the resurrection or say that Paul should be condemned because they believed in it as well.

(1) By Agrippa

Agrippa was probably thinking, "We know that it's all right to believe in the resurrection, but we don't believe that Jesus is the resurrected Messiah." Paul anticipated that.

(2) By the Jewish leaders

Paul also knew that many of the Jewish leaders believed in the resurrection, but that they wouldn't accept the resurrection of Jesus. Their disbelief is one of the most startling acts of willful rejection anywhere in Scripture. The resurrection has already occurred when Matthew 28:11-12 says, "Behold, some of the watch [the Roman soldiers who were guarding the tomb] came into the city, and showed unto the chief priests all the things that were done. And when they were assembled with the elders, and had taken counsel, they gave much money unto the soldiers." If you know anything about how the Jews hated the Romans, you know they wouldn't want to give them any money. Why did they do it? For bribery. They said, "Say ye, His disciples came by night, and stole him away while we slept" (v. 13). But if they were asleep, how could they possibly testify that the disciples stole the body? The chief priests bought the soldiers off. Then verses 14-15 say, "And if this come to the governor's ears, we will persuade him, and secure you. So they took the money, and did as they were taught; and this saying is commonly reported among the Jews until this day." Many still believe it even today.

4. His confession (vv. 9-11)

   a) Paul fought against Christ (v. 9)

   "I verily thought within myself, that I ought to do many things contrary to the name of Jesus of Nazareth."

   Paul could relate to what Agrippa was thinking. He tells him that he had the same problem: He thought it was right to do things contrary to the name of Jesus of Nazareth. Paul understood how Agrippa felt. That must have been devastating for Agrippa. Paul poured out his heart in confession, and I'm sure that was a painful thing for him to do. If anything in his life disturbed his conscience, it was that he had slaughtered Christians and compelled them to blaspheme

127

the name of Christ. Although he was redeemed, he always knew what he had done (1 Tim. 1:13-15).

b) Paul imprisoned Christians (v. 10)

"Which thing I also did in Jerusalem; and many of the saints did I shut up in prison, having received authority from the chief priests. And when they were put to death, I gave my voice against them."

The Greek word for "voice" referred to the little pebble that was used in the Sanhedrin for casting a vote. Paul was referring to his membership in the Sanhedrin and his voting in favor of the death of Christians.

c) Paul persecuted Christians (v. 11)

"And I punished them often in every synagogue, and compelled them to blaspheme [he tried to force Christians to recant their faith]; and being exceedingly mad against them, I persecuted them even unto foreign cities.

Paul was the chief officer of the Jewish inquisition. He was like a madman chasing Christians. The Bible says he was "breathing out threatenings and slaughter" (Acts 9:1). He hated and despised Christians and compelled them to blaspheme. No wonder he saw himself as the chief of sinners (1 Tim. 1:15). If the Christians wouldn't blaspheme, he made them martyrs.

Paul was saying, "Agrippa, I'm being condemned for believing what all Jews believe. But I know it's really for the sake of Jesus Christ. I know that's true because I used to hate Christ, and I didn't believe He was the Messiah. I went out under the authority of the Jewish leaders and slaughtered Christians."

5. His conversion (vv. 12-15)

Verse 12 begins the account of Paul's conversion. This is the high point of his testimony. He persecuted Christians to foreign cities, and one of them was Damascus.

a) Fighting a losing battle (vv. 12-14)

"Whereupon, as I went to Damascus with authority and commission from the chief priests, at midday, O king, I saw in the way a light from heaven, above the brightness of the sun, shining round about me and them who journeyed with me. And when we were all fallen to the earth, I heard a voice speaking unto me, and saying in the Hebrew tongue, Saul, Saul, why persecutest thou me? It is hard for thee to kick against the goads."

Jesus was saying, "Saul, give up; you can't win. Why are you continuing to do this against such odds?" The implication is that Paul was unsuccessful in trying to get Christians to blaspheme God. He was fighting something he was supposed to be submitting to. He was fighting a losing battle. You can imagine there wasn't a person on earth more miserable than Paul, trying to fight what he was supposed to submit to.

b) Submitting to Christ's lordship (v. 15)

"And I said, Who art thou, Lord? And he said, I am Jesus, whom thou persecutest."

Paul brought down a sledge hammer on the audience when he said, "I am Jesus, whom thou persecutest." That was Paul's conversion.

6. His commission (vv. 16-18)

a) Paul's calling (vv. 16-17)

"But rise, and stand upon thy feet; for I have appeared unto thee for this purpose, to make thee a minister and a witness both of these things which thou hast seen, and of those things in which I will appear unto thee; delivering thee from the people, and from the Gentiles, unto whom now I send thee."

(1) As an apostle

The Greek word for "send" is *apostellō*, from which we get the word *apostle*. Jesus made Paul an apostle.

(*a*) Appointed by the Lord

An apostle was someone who had to be personally appointed by the Lord Jesus Christ. The call of God to be an apostle involved a direct choice by our Lord. Paul was made an apostle by the Lord Himself. There are no apostles today because Christ is not here to appoint them. People are sent out to preach, but they are not apostles.

(b) An eyewitness of the resurrection

An apostle also had to be an eyewitness of the resurrected Christ. Acts 1:21-22 says, "Wherefore, of these men who have companied with us all the time that the Lord Jesus went in and out among us, beginning from the baptism of John unto that same day that he was taken up from us, must one be ordained to be a witness with us of his resurrection." Judas had been disqualified. The remaining disciples were trying to choose a replacement for Judas. Whomever they picked needed to have been a witness of the resurrected Christ. Acts 26:16 says that Jesus made Paul "a minister and a witness both of these things which thou has seen." Paul saw the glory of the Lord Jesus Christ. The resurrected Christ appeared to him on the Damascus road in brilliant glory brighter than the sun. At that time Jesus said this to Paul: "I will appear unto thee" (v. 16). Jesus appeared again to Paul in the Temple in Jerusalem while he was in a trance (Acts 22:17-21). Then He appeared to him again in the jail cell in Jerusalem when He told him he was going to go to Rome (Acts 23:11). He had seen the Lord at least three times by the time of Acts 25.

Paul fit the qualifications. He was called as an apostle.

(2) As a minister

Paul was also called as a minister and a witness. The concept of minister is a servant; a witness is someone who sees something and tells about it. Your testimony should come out of your own experience. In verse 17 Jesus speaks of Paul being delivered "from the people." "People" is a proper term referring to the Jewish people. And he was to be delivered "from the Gentiles [or pagans], unto whom now I send thee." Here is the cycle we are to follow: We were saved out of the world to go back into the world. Do you look at your job that way? When you go to work on

130

Monday morning, do you recognize yourself as having been commissioned by the Lord Jesus Christ as one sent to expose that community of people to the gospel of Christ and to transform them from darkness to light? You're a missionary. You may touch the world in a way that others cannot. You're an ambassador and have been committed to a ministry of reconciliation. You've been called to bring people into proper adjustment with God.

b) His message (v. 18)

(1) Conviction

"To open their eyes."

That is the starting point of the gospel. The first thing you have to do with unsaved people is open their eyes, because their eyes are blind. Israel's eyes were blind. Jesus said this about the Pharisees: "They are blind leaders of the blind. And if the blind lead the blind, both shall fall into the ditch" (Matt. 15:14). When the Word of God comes to men, they suddenly see what they never saw before. And what they usually see is sin. The key to opening a man's eyes is to uncover the blindness of sin. The Word of God opens men's eyes as the Holy Spirit convicts the world of sin, righteousness, and judgment (John 16:9-11). When we open men's eyes, we reveal the truth of salvation to them.

(2) Illumination

"To turn them from darkness to light."

(a) Living in darkness

A person without the Lord Jesus Christ lives in darkness. His mind is darkened, and he is alienated from God. Ephesians 4:18-19 says, "Having the understanding darkened, being alienated from the life of God through the ignorance that is in them, because of the blindness of their heart; who, being past feeling, have given themselves over unto lasciviousness, to work all uncleanness with greediness." That is the blindness of sin. Our objective is to use the Word of God to remove the scales of blindness and show them what is true. You can't truly evangelize unless you have some truth to reveal. Once the gospel opens men's eyes to the truth, it can transform them from darkness to light.

(b) Living in light

Salvation isn't about giving someone more light. Man doesn't need more light; he needs any light he can get. Unsaved man lives in darkness, and everything he does takes place in darkness. His understanding is dark, his will is dark—everything is dark. Salvation is an absolute transformation from the kingdom of darkness to the kingdom of God's dear Son (Col. 1:13). Paul calls it an inheritance of light in verse 12. When you walk in the light, you see things as they are. You can see the truth of God, and your path is clear. You can understand what God is doing and saying. And it all happens in a miraculous moment.

(3) Conversion

"From the power of Satan unto God."

Every man in the world is under the power of Satan or the power of God. There is no such thing as a free man. You have to choose who your master will be—either Satan or God. Many people think they are free to do what they want, but that's not true. Ephesians 2:1-2 says, "You hath he made alive, who were dead in trespasses and sins; in which in times past ye walked according to the course of this world, according to the prince of the power of the air, the spirit that now worketh in the children of disobedience" (KJV). Anyone who is disobedient to the gospel—any human being in the world other than a Christian—is guided by the spirit who works in him. And that spirit is the prince of the power of the air—Satan. Salvation means that you transfer from Satan's power to God's power. That's a total transformation. The unsaved man needs more than more information about God; he needs a total rebirth.

(4) Pardon

"That they may receive forgiveness of sins."

I can imagine that Agrippa and Bernice were squirming at about that point. Paul was a penetrating person. When he said they could receive forgiveness of sins, I can imagine him following that with a long stare and a long pause. Agrippa and Bernice knew enough to know that what they did was sin. They knew it not only because they knew the Old Testament but also because of their consciences. In a sense Paul was saying, "Forgiveness is available, Agrippa, for whatever you and Bernice have done." That's an exciting message to be able to give the world as the following verses confirm:

(*a*) 1 John 2:12—"Little children . . . your sins are forgiven you for his name's sake."

(*b*) Romans 4:8—"Blessed is the man to whom the Lord will not impute sin."

(*c*) Romans 8:33-34—"Who shall lay any thing to the charge of God's elect? Shall God that justifieth? . . . Shall Christ that died?" Will Christ accuse the one He died to save? No. Will Christ accuse you of the sin He died to bear on your behalf? No. There's no accusation against you. Forgiveness is full, free, and complete.

(5) Inheritance

"[An] inheritance among them who are sanctified."

The word translated "sanctified" means "holy." Another marvelous thing about becoming a Christian is the future promise of an inheritance undefiled and reserved in heaven for us (1 Pet. 1:4). We have an inheritance from God.

(6) Faith

"By faith that is in me."

On the day of Paul's conversion, Jesus told Paul to preach so he could open men's eyes and "turn them from darkness to light, and from the power of Satan unto God, that they may receive forgiveness of sins, and inheritance among them who are sanctified by faith that is in [Christ]" (v. 18). If any unbeliever would believe in Christ, salvation would be his. So Paul quoted to Agrippa the words of our Lord as they were given to Paul on the road to Damascus. There's only one way to know the truths of salvation, and that's by faith. The simple gospel of Jesus Christ that we're called to preach is in Ephesians 2:8-9: "For by grace are ye saved through faith; and that not of yourselves, it is the gift of God—not of works, lest any man should boast."

Paul is saying this to Agrippa: "I was a Jew of all the Jews. I was zealous not only for Judaism but also for killing Christians and trying to get them to blaspheme. One day I was walking on the Damascus road when a light shone in the middle of the day, brighter than the sun itself. It sent me to the ground, and I heard a voice. It said, 'Why don't you quit fighting me, Paul?' And I said, 'Who are you, Lord?' He was Jesus. Then He said to me, 'Arise, for I made you a minister and a witness.' Then He commissioned me to preach and told me what I was to say." In verse 19 Paul says, "Whereupon, O King Agrippa, I was not disobedient unto the heavenly vision." How could Paul disobey a voice from heaven?

Paul said he had been given the ministry of reconciliation (2 Cor. 5:18). Then he said, "We are ambassadors for Christ" (2 Cor. 5:20). We are to beg men to be reconciled to God. The word of reconciliation and the ministry of reconciliation have been committed to us. Will you be disobedient to that? Paul said he wasn't. I pray that you and I will not be disobedient, but that we too will be faithful to bring people into a right relationship with God. Our objective as we touch the lives of unsaved people is to convert them to Jesus Christ.

Focusing on the Facts

1. What kind of opportunity did Paul, Agrippa, and Festus see in the special hearing of Paul's case (see p. 114)?
2. What is boldness the result of (see p. 114)?
3. What motivated Paul to preach (2 Cor. 5:17; see p. 115)?
4. Define the ministry of reconciliation (2 Cor. 5:18; see pp. 115-16)?
5. What is an ambassador? Who are God's ambassadors? What is their responsibility (2 Cor. 5:20; see p. 116)?

6. What is one of God's purposes in saving people out of the world (Acts 26:17; see p. 117)?
7. What do Christians have a tendency to forget when they become satisfied with learning, fellowship, and growth (see pp. 117-18)?
8. Why was Paul happy to give his testimony before Agrippa (Acts 26:2-3; see pp. 118-19)?
9. Upon what did Paul center his testimony (see p. 119)?
10. Why did Paul use a double superlative in Acts 26:5 (see p. 120)?
11. What was the hope that Paul was being judged for? Explain (Acts 26:6; see pp. 120-21).
12. Although most of the Jewish leaders believed in the resurrection, what wouldn't they accept (see p. 122)?
13. Why could Paul relate to Agrippa's thinking about Christ (Acts 26:9; see pp. 122-23)?
14. How successful was Paul in his attempts to make Christians blaspheme Christ (Acts 26:14; see p. 124)?
15. Describe the two necessary qualifications for an apostle of Christ (see pp. 124-25).
16. What is the first thing that must happen with any unsaved person before he can receive the gospel? Explain (Acts 26:18; see p. 126).
17. Who is the guide of those who are disobedient to the gospel (Eph. 2:1-2; see p. 127)?
18. What is the only way that one can know the truths of salvation (see p. 129)?

Pondering the Principles

1. Read 2 Corinthians 5:17-21. According to Paul, all Christians have been given the ministry of reconciliation. What are some ways that you can be involved as an ambassador for Christ? Make a list of people you know whom you would like to see brought into proper adjustment with God. Begin praying that God would use you in bringing about their reconciliation to Him.

2. Have you become comfortable in your Christian walk? That is, do you find that Bible study, strong fellowship with other belivers, and growth in your spiritual life are all you need to do to be fulfilled as a Christian? Read Ephesians 6:19-20. What was Paul's commitment? Remember that God saved you so He could send you into the world with His message. How do you need to change your priorities to reflect God's plan in reaching the world for Christ?

3. Read Acts 26:18. Review the six aspects of God's commission to Paul (see pp. 126-29). How many of those six things do you discuss when you share the gospel with someone? As a way of reminder, recall your conversion experience and determine how each of those six aspects fit it. Remember to share your testimony and emphasize those six aspects when you do. Thank God for His message of salvation. Pray that He might use you to communicate the gospel the same way He did through Paul.

8
Paul Before Agrippa—Part 3
Are You Trying to Convert Me?

Outline

Review
I. The Consultation of Paul's Testimony (25:13-22)
II. The Circumstances of Paul's Testimony (25:23-27)
III. The Commencement of Paul's Testimony (26:1-18)

Lesson
IV. The Culmination of Paul's Testimony (26:19-23)
    A. His Commitment (vv. 19-20)
        1. The principle of submission (v. 19)
        2. The practice of submission (v. 20)
    B. His Capture (v. 21)
    C. His Continuance (vv. 22-23)
        1. Confidence in God (v. 22*a*)
        2. Confidence in the gospel (vv. 22*b*-23)
V. The Consequence of Paul's Testimony (vv. 24-32)
    A. The Interruption (v. 24)
    B. The Invitation (vv. 25-29)
        1. Paul's incisive reasoning (vv. 25-27)
            a) Wisdom (v. 25)
            b) Truth (v. 26)
            c) Knowledge (v. 27)
        2. Agrippa's incredulous response (v. 28)
        3. Paul's intimate restraint (v. 29)
    C. The Impact (vv. 30-32)
        1. Paul's innocence affirmed (v. 30-31)
        2. Paul's message avoided (v. 32)
            a) The hindrance of popularity
            b) The honor of faithfulness

Lesson

IV. THE CULMINATION OF PAUL'S TESTIMONY (26:19-23)

In any act of God's sovereignty, it is necessary that there be a response of the human will. God does not hit people over the head with a sovereign hammer; there must be an act of the will. And that was true in the case of Paul.

A. His Commitment (vv. 19-20)

1. The principle of submission (v. 19)

"Whereupon, O King Agrippa, I was not disobedient unto the heavenly vision."

Once Paul realized that Jesus of Nazareth was the living Messiah, he submitted his will. That is a necessary part of commitment. There must be obedience. Salvation is a sovereign act of God, but it also involves a human response. In Galatians 1:16 Paul says that when the Lord called him into the ministry, he "conferred not with flesh and blood" but immediately began to do what God had called him to do. He didn't seek human wisdom; he responded to God in instant obedience. That is the response God asks for.

The response of obedience is an important part of the paradox of sovereignty and responsibility. God acts sovereignly to carry out His will, but He demands a human response within the framework of that sovereignty. When you give your testimony you don't say, "One day I was walking along, and I was suddenly saved in an instant. One moment I didn't know what a Christian was, now I am one." It isn't that simple. There had to be an act of your will for salvation to occur. When you give your testimony you say, "One day I committed myself to the Lord Jesus Christ." You were saved consciously, as an act of your will. Yet the Bible says that salvation is a sovereign act of God designed before the world began (Eph. 1:4). Both are true. The sovereign life of Christ is lived through you, but you need to submit your will to allow Him to live through you. God sovereignly motivates your will, but it has to be activated. God ultimately knows what will happen, and He will accomplish His work; but Paul said he was obedient. That is the most important thing in the Christian life—the submission of your will to God.

Principles of Obedience

1. Obedience is a mark of conversion

    First Peter 1:14 says that you ought to walk "as obedient children." Romans 6:16 says, "Know ye not that to whom ye yield yourselves servants to obey, his servants ye are whom ye obey?" If you've yielded yourself to the Lord Jesus Christ, whom then should you obey? The Lord Jesus Christ. Obedience is a mark of conversion. If you're God's child, you'll obey what He says.

2. Obedience is a recognition of authority

    When you obey, you are telling God that He is in control and that you are in submission to Him. When you do not obey God, you are playing God—you have usurped divine authority. If you know clearly that God wants you to do something, and you don't do it, then you have replaced God as the controlling authority in your life. Yet that's what we do most of the time. In Acts 5:29 Peter says, "We ought to obey God rather than men." You have that choice. Perhaps God has spoken to your heart many times about serving in a particular ministry, but you said no. When you said that, you replaced God as the sovereign ruler of your life.

3. Obedience is a characteristic of faith

    Hebrews 11:8 says that Abraham obeyed God by faith. When you believe God, you'll obey Him because you know He has your best interests at heart. When you disobey, you are actually saying, "God, You don't know what's best for me. I don't trust You." When you disobey God, you're not trusting Him. Abraham was willing to go to the Promised Land without knowing anything because He trusted God. Every time you disobey God, you're telling Him that He's not worthy of your trust—and that's blasphemy.

4. Obedience is a proof of love

Don't tell God you love Him unless you obey. Jesus said, "If ye love me, keep my commandments" (John 14:15). Then He said, "He that hath my commandments, and keepeth them, he it is that loveth me" (John 14:21).

Obedience is a mark of conversion, a recognition of authority, a characteristic of faith, and a proof of love. Obedience is the prerequisite to power and effectiveness. A disobedient Christian is useless.

Paul was not disobedient; he had to submit. The living Messiah commanded him from out of heaven.

2. The practice of submission (v. 20)

"But showed first unto them of Damascus, and at Jerusalem, and throughout all the borders of Judaea, and then to the Gentiles, that they should repent and turn to God, and do works fit for repentance."

Salvation becomes apparent by the works that believers practice. James said that he could know if someone's faith was real by their works (James 2:18). Matthew 7:16 says, "Ye shall know them by their fruits."

Paul indicated to Agrippa that Christianity is the logical and necessary sequel to Judaism's past. The central hope of the Jew was the resurrection and a living Messiah. The resurrected One spoke to Paul, who saw His glory and heard His voice. He could do nothing but obey. Christ commissioned Paul into His ministry, and he obeyed instantly. He began at Damascus, then in Jerusalem, and then into the borders of Judea. Afterwards, he went on three journeys into the Gentile world. He preached about repentance and doing works that prove one's repentance is real.

B. His Capture (v. 21)

"For these causes the Jews caught me in the temple, and went about to kill me."

The Jews wanted Paul dead because he was offering equal salvation to Gentiles. They couldn't tolerate equality with Gentiles. So they tried to kill him while he was in the Temple.

That's how he became a prisoner.

The true gospel cannot be presented unless the importance of repentance is emphasized. Verse 18 says that the first thing Paul was to do was to open people's eyes. That involves conviction of sin and turning from sin. There can be no legitimate salvation when there is no turning from sin. There must be a transformation. A person who is truly saved will set aside his sinful patterns. Because Paul offered salvation equally to Gentiles and to Jews, the Jewish leaders caught him in the Temple and tried to kill him.

C. His Continuance (vv. 22-23)

1. Confidence in God (v. 22a)

"Having, therefore, obtained help from God."

Paul was always getting help from God. In 2 Corinthians 1:8-10 he says he endured trouble that almost took his life, but the Lord helped and delivered him. He wrote to Timothy about how God delivered him (2 Tim. 3:11; 4:17-18). He constantly was being helped by God as he ministered. That is a promise the minister can depend on. If God calls you to a ministry, He will sustain and undergird you with His own strength to accomplish His will. People often say to me, "John, how can you do so many things?" I have help from the Lord. I believe the Lord strengthens me when I need strength and gives me wisdom when I need wisdom. I believe that if God puts you in a position, He will support you in that position. You can step out and do what you sense God is leading you to do when you have the confidence that He'll support you. The Lord helped Paul even though the Jewish leaders wanted to kill him.

2. Confidence in the gospel (vv. 22b-23)

"I continue unto this day, witnessing both to small and great, saying no other things than those which the prophets and Moses did say should come: that Christ should suffer, and that he should be the first [Gk., *prōtos*; not the first in chronological order but in preeminence] that should rise from the dead, and should show light unto the people, and to the Gentiles."

Paul continued to preach equal salvation to Jew and Gentile. And he continued to have help from God to preach that the Messiah would have to suffer. That's in the Old Testament in Psalm 22 and Isaiah 53. His rising from the dead is prophesied in Psalm 16:10, "Neither wilt thou suffer thine Holy One to see corruption" (KJV). Paul continued to preach what the Old Testament taught.

This is essentially what Paul said to Agrippa: "I've been changed. I've been turned into a minister of Jesus Christ by a sovereign act of the living Christ. I submitted myself to Him, and now I'm proclaiming Him. People have tried to shut my mouth by attempts on my life, but they haven't succeeded. Here I am two years later saying the same thing I said then and saying it just as boldly today. There is an equal salvation to both Jew and Gentile." Saying that took courage.

V. THE CONSEQUENCE OF PAUL'S TESTIMONY (vv. 24-32)

A. The Interruption (v. 24)

"And as he thus spoke for himself, Festus said with a loud voice, Paul, thou art beside thyself; much learning doth make thee mad."

Today, we think much learning makes people intelligent. In that day, they had a different view of education. Festus told Paul that he was over-educated—that too much learning had made him go insane. What made Festus say that? Because of what Paul says in verse 23: that Christ should rise from the dead. Festus could not understand the concept of the resurrection. He thought only one kind of man babbled about visions, revelations, voices out of heaven, and resurrections, and that was a crazy man. Festus had to acknowledge that Paul was intelligent, but a Roman with any reasoning ability would have difficulty in believing all that he taught. Festus's interruption set the stage for what Paul wanted to say next.

B. The Invitation (vv. 25-29)

1. Paul's incisive reasoning (vv. 25-27)

a) Wisdom (v. 25)

"But he said, I am not mad, most noble Festus, but speak forth the words of truth and soberness."

The word translated "soberness" is *sōphrosunē* in the Greek text. The prefix *sōph* is derived from the word *sophia*, which means "wisdom" or "total control of the senses." Paul spoke with total control of his senses—with a sound mind.

142

b)   Truth (v. 26)

"For the king knoweth of these things, before whom also I speak freely; for I am persuaded that none of these things are hidden from him; for this thing was not done in a corner."

Paul is telling Festus that he isn't mad, but that he is speaking with a clear mind and that King Agrippa knew he spoke the truth. The thing that was "not done in a corner" was the death and resurrection of Christ. It was common knowledge. Everyone knew that Jesus had lived and died and that there was a claim to His resurrection.

Paul was brilliant in his reasoning. He presented the gospel to Agrippa and now forces him to come to a conclusion that he probably wouldn't have made on his own. He turns Agrippa into a silent witness to Festus. The king hadn't said a word but by that very fact was attesting that what Paul said was true. The case was clear, and the king knew it. Anyone who believed in the prophets, Moses, and historical facts would have to conclude that Jesus of Nazareth is the Messiah. And Agrippa would have to make that conclusion.

c)   Knowledge (v. 27)

"King Agrippa, believest thou the prophets? I know that thou believest."

Paul was telling Agrippa that if he believed the prophets, he would have to believe that Jesus is the Messiah. He knew the truth. Paul made Agrippa responsible. On one particular occasion when I was sharing Christ with someone, I said, "Now that you've heard the gospel you're responsible, because you know the truth. You may reject it at this time, but God holds you responsible for the truth you know." Paul was trying to capture Agrippa's will. He wanted Agrippa to do what he had done himself—make the logical conclusion that Jesus is the Messiah.

Agrippa was now in a bind. If he said, "I do believe the prophets," then he would be tacitly admitting that Jesus is the Messiah. That would put him in deep trouble with the Jewish leaders. But if he said, "I don't believe the prophets," then he would be in even deeper trouble with them. So he couldn't say yes or no.

2. Agrippa's incredulous response (v. 28)

"Then Agrippa said unto Paul, Almost thou persuadest me to be a Christian."

The King James Version doesn't capture what Agrippa said. The Greek text should be translated: "In such a short time are you trying to convert me?" Agrippa avoided the question.

3. Paul's intimate restraint (v. 29)

"And Paul said, I would to God that not only thou but also all that hear me this day were both almost, and altogether, such as I am, except these bonds."

That's a confusing verse, so let me give you the best translation: "Whether in a short or long time, I would to God that not only you but also all who have been with me this day might become such as I am, except for these chains." Whether it was a short or long time, Paul was trying to convert Agrippa and everyone else. Then he added that he wished them to be like himself, except for the chains. Paul had a gentle and honest approach to them. He wasn't bitter over his circumstances. He didn't say, "You ought to have these chains, and I ought to be sitting on that throne!" Paul wanted them to know the liberty he had in his soul, not the physical chains he wore. Paul looked at all those people in fancy dress and told them that he wished they were like he was. They had everything in the world, but they really had nothing. Jesus said, "What shall it profit a man, if he shall gain the whole world, and lose his own soul? Or what shall a man give in exchange for his soul?" (Mark 8:36-37). Paul was probably willing to die to save Agrippa, but he wouldn't wish his chains on him. That's the heart of the Christian. That's evangelism with love. How could anyone resist that kind of message spoken with such concern and love?

C. The Impact (vv. 30-32)

1. Paul's innocence affirmed (vv. 30-31)

"When he had thus spoken, the king rose up, and the governor, and Bernice, and they that sat with them; and when they were gone aside, they talked between themselves, saying, This man doeth nothing worthy of death or of bonds."

Paul was innocent. The Holy Spirit included this verse to show that the king of Palestine and the governor from Rome both agreed that Paul was innocent. Christianity is not insurrection, heresy, or political treason; it is a spiritual relationship to the living God. People have accused true Christianity of all kinds of atrocity, and it isn't so. True Christianity is guilty of nothing worthy of death or bonds. It's great that they judged him to be innocent, but what about their personal spiritual responses?

2. Paul's message avoided (v. 32)

"Then said Agrippa unto Festus, This man might have been set at liberty, if he had not appealed unto Caesar."

They could have decided to let him go. There wasn't any need to appeal to Caesar. There wasn't any case. Caesar hadn't heard a word about it. There hadn't even been a letter written. But Festus and Agrippa hid behind the appeal of Paul. Although a man can have the gospel directed right at him, he is lost unless he activates his will.

a) The hindrance of popularity

What hindered Agrippa and Festus? Since Paul was innocent, why would they push the case to Rome, hiding behind his appeal? Because the most important things to them were popularity and their immoral life-styles. Agrippa was vile, self-centered, unbelieving, prideful, ignorant, and indifferent. Those traits are the same things that hinder other people from receiving Christ.

b) The honor of faithfulness

The rejection of the gospel message didn't discourage Paul. People could believe him, or people could curse him, but he didn't change. When he made it to Rome, the first thing he did was to preach Jesus. People will say to me, "I've tried to share Christ, but there doesn't seem to be any response." But that's all right, because God didn't call you to save people; he called you to preach Christ. God does the saving. All He asks of you is to be faithful. Paul's passion and dominant spirit could not be squelched. He continued to be faithful. Why? Because his service was for

God and not based on man's response. It wasn't up to him to determine the results. He preached to a great crowd, and no one responded positively, but that didn't change him. May we be like him.

Focusing on the Facts

1. Although salvation is a sovereign act of God, what must it also involve (see p. 133)?
2. Explain the paradox involved in the salvation of an individual (see p. 134).
3. What are four principles of obedience? Explain each one (see pp. 134-35).
4. How does salvation in one's life become apparent (Acts 26:20; see p. 135)?
5. What needs to be emphasized if the true gospel is to be presented (see p. 136)?
6. What promise can those who are called into the ministry depend on (see p. 136)?
7. Why did Festus think Paul was mad? What didn't Festus understand (Acts 26:24; see p. 137)?
8. How did Paul turn Agrippa into a silent witness to the truth of what he said (Acts 26:26; see pp. 137-38)?
9. Explain Paul's gentle appraoch to Agrippa and Festus (Acts 26:29; see p. 138).
10. How did Agrippa and Festus avoid the truth of Paul's message (see p. 140)?
11. Why wasn't Paul discouraged when his message was rejected (see p. 140)?

Pondering the Principles

1. What is your reaction when you present the gospel and someone rejects it? Does that reaction affect your willingness to continue to share the good news with the unsaved? God has called you to share Christ with the unsaved, but you are not responsible for saving them. With that in mind, what should your attitude be when you communicate the gospel? Ask God to give you boldness as you approach people. Thank Him that he has the responsibility for bringing people to Himself. Make it your goal to communicate the gospel whenever you have the opportunity.

2. Reread the principles of obedience (see pp. 134-35). Take a good look at your Christian life, and ask yourself if you habitually seek

to obey God. Is obedience really important to you, or do you usually obey God only when it is convenient? Remember, Jesus said that the one who truly loves Him will obey Him. Memorize John 14:15: "If you love Me, you will keep My commandments" (NASB).

Scripture Index